Studies in Economic Growth, No.15

General Editor: **A.M. Khusro**

BANGLA DESH ECONOMY : PROBLEMS AND PROSPECTS

सत्यमेव परमो धर्म :

Institute of Economic Growth

INSTITUTE OF ECONOMIC GROWTH
STUDIES IN ECONOMIC GROWTH

INSTITUTE OF ECONOMIC GROWTH, DELHI

BANGLA DESH ECONOMY
Problems and Prospects

Edited by
V.K.R.V. RAO

VIKAS PUBLICATIONS
DELHI - BOMBAY - BANGALORE
KANPUR - LONDON

VIKAS PUBLICATIONS

5 Daryaganj, Ansari Road, Delhi-6
Savoy Chambers, 5 Wallace Street, Bombay-1
10 First Main Road, Gandhi Nagar, Bangalore-9
80 Canning Road, Kanpur
17-21 Sunbeam Road, North Acton, London NW 10

SBN 7069 0177 0

PRINTED IN INDIA

AT DELHI PRESS, RANI JHANSI ROAD, JHANDEWALA ESTATE,
NEW DELHI, AND PUBLISHED BY MRS SHARDA CHAWLA,
VIKAS PUBLICATIONS, 5 DARYAGANJ, ANSARI ROAD, DELHI-6

PREFACE

This brief study of some of the economic aspects of Bangla Desh owes its origin to a panel discussion which I organized on "The Economic Prospects of Bangla Desh". The discussion was held under the joint auspices of the Institute of Economic Growth and the India International Centre, and participants included Professor Arjun Sengupta, P.C. Verma, Dr B.B. Bhattacharya, Dr A.M. Khusro and Professor Boudhayan Chattopadhyay, with myself acting as Chairman. Subsequently, and on the request of some friends, I agreed that it would be useful and serve a larger public if the papers read at the meeting were to be published in book form together with some available basic statistics on Bangla Desh. My opening speech and the paper by Dr Khusro are published as delivered at the meeting. The papers by P.C. Verma and Dr B.B. Bhattacharya are revised versions, while those by Dr P.C. Joshi and Dr B.N. Ganguli have been specially contributed for this volume at my request. Professor Arjun Sengupta, who had already published some articles on Bangla Desh economics and had subsequently written more on the basis of his panel contribution, preferred, and I think rightly and with profit both for the subject as well as for the reader, to have included in the volume both his articles on the subject. My fresh contribution is an editorial introduction that sums up the substance of the papers as also of the panel discussion. A brief appendix is added at the end of the volume.

It is the hope of all the contributors and of the Institute of

Economic Growth that has organized this study, that it will
enlighten the general reader on the economic background
underlying the Bangla Desh struggle for national liberation,
the problems that now face independent Bangla Desh and
also give him a view on the economic prospects of this gallant
new nation on the Indian subcontinent.

V.K.R.V.Rao
Institute of Economic Growth

CONTENTS

CONTRIBUTORS

BHATTACHARYA, B.B.
Junior Fellow, Institute of Economic Growth, Delhi

CHATTOPADHYAY, BOUDHAYAN
Associate Professor of Economics, Jawaharlal Nehru University, New Delhi

GANGULI, B.N.
Emeritus Professor and Former Vice-Chancellor, University of Delhi, Delhi

JOSHI, P.C.
Senior Fellow, Institute of Economic Growth, Delhi

KHUSRO, A.M.
Director, Institute of Economic Growth, Delhi, and Professor of Economics, University of Delhi, Delhi

RAO, V.K.R.V.
Honorary Fellow, Institute of Economic Growth, Delhi; Director, Institute for Social and Economic Change, Bangalore, and Member Parliament

SENGUPTA, ARJUN
Reader, Delhi School of Economics, University of Delhi; Recently appointed Economic Counsellor, Indian Mission in Dacca, Bangla Desh

VERMA, P.C.
Junior Fellow, Institute of Economic Growth, Delhi

V.K.R.V. RAO

INTRODUCTION

THE TEN PAPERS included in this volume give a succinct and well-documented picture of the economic maltreatment of Bangla Desh when it was a part of Pakistan and the problems that now face that country in its task of rehabilitation, reconstruction, and development. The subject thus naturally divides itself into two logical parts, one dealing with the past, and the other with the present and possible glimpses into the future.

Both Professor Arjun Sengupta and P.C. Verma deal with the economic history of Bangla Desh when it was a part of Pakistan and the manner in which its differential treatment brought about disparity and laid the foundations for the economic despair which was part-cause of the movement that brought liberation to the people of East Bengal. The first thing to note is that Pakistan came into being in 1947 with a western and an eastern wing, the initial position regarding the economic position and potential of the two wings did not present any significant difference. Both the wings were almost wholly agricultural economies with hardly any modern industries and relying on imports for their requirements of manufactures whether of consumer or of capital goods. Such external trade as they had was with that part of the subcontinent which became the Republic of India and there was practically no trade between the two wings of Pakistan. Nor was there any significant difference in their agricultural potential, though the technical problems involved in the realization of this potential was not the same in the two wings. It is true that the western wing did have some initial advantage over its eastern wing, as it had received a better deal when it was in the old Punjab than the eastern wing had when it was a part of the old Bengal. Nevertheless, it is also a fact that the initial disparities were no more than marginal, as can be seen by a reference to the statistical appendix. Professor Sengupta is therefore quite right when he says that "when Pakistan was created in 1947, there was little in the nature of its economy which could have indicated the way its western wing could grow to dominate its eastern part. If one looked into the details of the initial conditions of Pakistan's development, in terms of factor endowments, resource position or growth potential, one could not seriously maintain that it was in the nature of things that West Pakistan should dominate the East or that a different set of policies could not have achieved quite a different pattern of regional development.

The difference in treatment of the two wings began almost from the very inception of Pakistan. With practically no industrial background, Pakistan had to depend upon imported raw materials and machinery for its intermediate and investment industries, while in the case of consumer industries and other industries based on domestic raw materials, machinery had to be imported from abroad. With a system of import licensing and foreign exchange allocation, much depended upon Government policy in determining both the location and growth of industries in Pakistan. With the eastern wing contributing the bulk of the country's foreign exchange surplus, one would normally have expected a much higher rate of industrial growth in that part of the country. In actual practice, and as a result of the deliberate pro-west wing and anti-east wing policy adopted by the central Government of Pakistan, the foreign exchange surplus generated by East Pakistan was mainly used for bringing about the industrial development of West Pakistan except to the extent that development of jute manufactures was promoted in East Pakistan to bring about a further increase in the foreign exchange surplus that could be used for West Pakistan. Apart from the direct absorption of East Pakistan's foreign exchange surplus for the development of West Pakistan, a part of this surplus was also drained off to West Pakistan by the sale of its manufactures to East Pakistan which had acquired an internal and sheltered market. In addition, almost the whole of the foreign aid received by Pakistan in the earlier years and a major portion in subsequent years was used for the development of West Pakistan. This can be seen from the statistics of foreign trade surplus and deficit of the two wings during the period of 1950-51 to 1959-60 given in Professor Sengupta's paper. Thus, during these 10 years of the fifties East Pakistan generated a foreign trade surplus of Rs 389.5 crores. Of this amount, Rs 223 crores went to the credit of West Pakistan to pay for the goods it exported to East Pakistan and the import surplus that East Pakistan had thus accumulated with West Pakistan. That the balance of the foreign trade surplus of East Pakistan and the bulk of foreign aid received by Pakistan was also used up for West Pakistan can be seen from the fact that during this period, West Pakistan had a foreign trade deficit of Rs 554.5 crores, while in its intra-regional trade with East Pakistan it had a surplus

of Rs 229.9 crores.   This left it with a net foreign exchange
deficit of Rs 331.6 crores of which Rs 166.6 crores or about
half was met by using the foreign exchange surplus of East
Pakistan and the other half by foreign aid.   "In any case",
Professor Sengupta says, "it is clear that a substantial part
of the resources generated in East Pakistan during this period,
which could have been used within that province, were transferred to West Pakistan to finance a large fraction of the
total absorption of resources in West Pakistan over and above
what was generated in that region."

The second point to note is that during these 10 years ending
with 1959-60 the distribution of developmental expenditure
under the plan was very much to the disadvantage of East
Pakistan.   Thus out of the Rs 346.6 crores spent on planned
development, the share of East Pakistan was only Rs 105.6
cores or less than 31 per cent, and per capita expenditure about
one-third of that in West Pakistan. The result was a big disparity
in the development of infra-structure facilities in the two
wings, power production in terms of Kwh being only 2.3 per
capita in East Pakistan as compared to 20.2 in West Pakistan.
Some of the other differences in developmental facilities that
emerged at the end of this period, that is in 1959-60, are given
by Professor Sengupta in the table on the next page.

The third point of significance is the larger volume of
private investment in West Pakistan which was due partly to
the discrimination in infra-structural facilities, commercial
and industrial licences, foreign exchange allocations, and general governmental support including public expenditure.
In fact, private investment in West Pakistan was two to nearly
three times that in East Pakistan and this was the natural
effect of increasing the disparity in economic growth between

Item	Unit	East Pakistan	West Pakistan
Railway wagons	Number per million persons	6	166
Buses and trucks	—do—	85	495
Post offices	—do—	83	186
High-type roads	Metres per million persons	28	225
Branch offices of banks	Number per million persons	110	286
Industrial licence imports	Value as percentage of total for Pakistan	35	65
Commercial licence imports	—do—	36	64
Value added in large scale manufacture	Rs in crores	39	116

the two wings. Thus, according to the figures in the statistical appendix, private investment in East Pakistan during this period was only Rs 237.0 crores as against Rs 537.0 crores in West Pakistan. This was further aggravated by the disparity in public expenditure. According to Professor Sengupta, public expenditure during the period amounted to about Rs 763 crores of which Rs 600 crores or about 79 per cent went to West Pakistan. This great difference between East and West Pakistan in respect of both private investment and public expenditure naturally led to a great and growing disparity in the growth rates between the two wings.

A belated attempt was made during the succeeding decade comprising Pakistan's second and third plan periods to bring about some rectification by increasing the quantum of public expenditure in East Pakistan. Even then it fell short of the increased expenditure that was simultaneously also being incurred in West Pakistan. The natural forces set in motion by the wide disparities in public expenditure during the first 10 years, coupled with the other features of government policy, referred to earlier, made for the persistence of wide disparities between the two wings in respect of private investment. Thus, according to the figures given by P.C. Verma, though private investment in East Pakistan during the second ten years showed a larger total of Rs 856 crores, that in West Pakistan was much larger and stood at Rs 2662 crores, giving it a share of about 76 per cent of the combined Pakistan total. The result was a continuance and widening of the disparity between the two wings over the entire period during which what is now Bangla Desh had remained as East Pakistan. This is best summed up in P.C. Verma's paper when he points out that in two decades 1949-50 to 1969-70, per capita income in East Pakistan rose only by 0.7 per cent a year, while the rate of increase in West Pakistan was 2.0 per cent or nearly three times that in Pakistan. The result was that though the two wings started with practically the same per capita income or at best with a marginal difference in favour of West Pakistan, the disparity between their per capita incomes grew apace, with per capita income in Bangla Desh standing at Rs 339 in 1969-70, while the corresponding figure for West Pakistan was Rs 500. The difference amounted to 33 per cent in favour of West Pakistan if we took the West Pakistan figure as base or 50 per cent in disfavour of East Pakistan if one took East Pakistan as base. Details of the disparities under different heads are given in the statistical appendix which has been prepared by P.C. Verma.

Before concluding this part of my introduction, I must also draw attention to the additional economic distress caused to East Pakistan which has been pointed out both by Professor Sengupta and several other contributors to this volume. This was the result of the higher value of the Pakistani rupee in West Pakistan as compared to that in East Pakistan. Prices of the basic foodgrains were higher in East Pakistan while the prices of its imported manufactures from West Pakistan were also higher not only because of the long transport haul but also because of the virtually monopolistic character of these imports and the forced lack of competition from neighbouring countries like India. This meant a further exploitation of East Pakistan by West Pakistan and was the result not only of its being a part of Pakistan but also because of the anti-India posture of the central Government which had, as pointed out in my opening address to the panel discussion, much more adverse consequences on its eastern wing than on its western wing. Altogether, it is clear that though East Bengal had the legal status of being a part of Pakistan and therefore entitled to fair and equal treatment, it was in fact treated more or less as a colonial appendage of West Pakistan and thus in addition to the cultural and other discrimination it suffered at the hands of its West Pakistani rulers.

The rest of the volume deals with the problems that independent Bangla Desh faces now and the possible measures that could be adopted to deal with them. Dr P.C. Joshi focuses his main attention on the subject of agrarian relations and the need for giving priority to the implementation of suitable land reforms. Dr Ganguli deals with a larger canvas, though he also concentrates his attention on the agricultural problems of Bangla Desh. He writes of the need for giving immediate attention to agriculture, fisheries, poultry farming, animal husbandry and plantation agriculture in Bangla Desh, the importance of devising new agricultural varieties to suit the climatic and other special natural features of that state, and the possibilities of joint work by India and Bangla Desh on the development of inland waterways in the eastern region of the subcontinent.

Dr B.B. Bhattacharya has contributed an excellent and well documented paper on the external trade, past and possible future, of Bangla Desh. After giving a detailed account of how the rulers of Pakistan followed a commercial policy aimed at utilizing the surplus of East Pakistan, restricting its foreign imports and creating a sheltered market therein for West Pakistani imports, he deals with the possible and beneficial changes that could emerge in the trade structure of Bangla Desh as a result of its liberation. He rightly points out the difficult nature of the jute problem that will now emerge with India and Bangla Desh functioning in their new relationship of mutual regard and cooperation and suggests the possibility of the two countries settling up a jute community to handle their combined problem of jute exports. The same suggestion is also made by Professor B. Chattopadhyay. Dr Bhattacharya also discusses the possibility of India providing both an alternative market and an alternative source of supply for the change that may take place in the exports and imports of Bangla Desh in view of its strained relations with West Pakistan. He also stresses, and rightly, the need for Bangla Desh to step up its production of paper, newsprint and timber and for diversifying its agriculture to include increased production of raw cotton and oil seeds. Dr Khusro confines his attention to the underlying criteria that should be followed by India in developing its trade and investment relations with Bangla Desh rather than the details of its trade and investment prospects. He stresses the importance of India encouraging the continuation and expansion of the current exports of Bangla Desh to the rest of the world and warns India against trying to replace its imports of manufactures from West Pakistan by Indian supplies except to the extent that these cannot be domestically produced in Bangla Desh with the encouragement and support of its now independent Government. While he is not against resuming the pre-partition trade with East Bengal, which is now Bangla Desh, he would put in a strong qualification, namely that this should be done "only if comparative advantages still lie in that direction".

Dr Khusro also warns us to go warily in seeking investment outlets in Bangla Desh, refers to the experience we have had both with tied foreign aid and with foreign private investment, and suggests that, lines of credit, if extended, should be on a government-to-government basis rather than through private sources. He would also prefer India to aid Bangla Desh through her scientific laboratories and research organizations rather than by sending technical personnel who will be expecting big salaries on UN scales. In this context, I may draw attention to the suggestion I have made in the address referred to earlier of the possibility of constituting a Bangla Desh development corps in India "consisting of young volunteers with different types of technical, scientific and developmental skills, whose services could be used by the Government of

Bangla Desh and who would take a remuneration that would only cover their living expenses". But as Dr Khusro has emphasized, the entire responsibility for getting either investment or technology or technical or other personnel should be entirely that of the Government of Bangla Desh and should have no colour of any attempt at extending Indian influence in that country.

Professor Sengupta begins his contribution to the subject by the caution that India's own potential is limited and her ability to help in Bangla Desh reconstruction is small. He points out that "our relations with them can be neither of aid-givers nor of advisers. These have to be based on mutual help and benefits of trade and economic relations." He first deals with the immediate problems that face Bangla Desh and emphasizes in this connection the availability of foodgrains and the proper and efficient distribution of whatever is or can be made available. His paper contains a good analysis of the food problem of Bangla Desh, explains why famine has not broken out in that state in spite of nine months of war and destruction, and why the problem may, in the absence of supplementary supplies from outside, not assume serious dimensions because of the return of refugees, increase in purchasing power, and restoration of peace and normal living in that country. He suggests a substantial programme of imports, a big programme of domestic procurement and the immediate introduction of rationing throughout Bangla Desh. Fortunately, the people of Bangla Desh have learnt to live with wheat consumption during the last few years of their association with West Pakistan and, even more fortunately, India is currently in a position to spare substantial quantities of wheat for their use. Also relevant in this connection is the need for quick rehabilitation, if not expansion, of transport facilities for the efficient distribution of domestically procured and imported foodgrains. In the second part of his paper, Professor Sengupta traces the problems that will rise with the attempts at reconstruction and points to the special need for preventing private trade from profiteering. He also calls for a nationalization of banking and adds that "the whole banking structure will have to be rebuilt, the entire method of operation will have to be charged, and the norms of behaviour will have to be geared to activities that have long-run social benefits". He then deals with the immediate needs of Bangla Desh agriculture in terms of fertilizers, pesticides, and credit. Referring to manufactures, he points out that the immediate problem is one of getting production activities moving again and the need for immediate repairs to damaged plants, import of destroyed items, and the giving of credit and confidence to those in charge of production. Professor Sengupta rightly refers to the need for matching physical requirements with financial flows and the need for careful choice in setting the parameters of government action including the public sector and control of the private sector. He concludes with the hope that notwithstanding the difficulties facing Bangla Desh, its newly won independence would generate the sacrifice and dedicated effort that could solve its problem of economic reconstruction.

The last paper in this section is contributed by Professor Chattopadhyay and covers a much wider compass than any of the previous contributors to this volume. As the title of his paper indicates, the subject dealt with is not only the reconstruction of Bangla Desh but also the related reconstruction of India. Professor Chattopadhyay is of the

firm view that steps must be taken to prevent the export
to Bangla Desh of what he terms the Indian type of capital
accumulation with its emphasis on foreign capital collaboration, extent of foreign control, pervasiveness of monopoly in
the economy and the Indian businessman's penchant for
making quick profits. He would therefore suggest that India
should reform her own system of capital accumulation by
nationalizing her jute industry, giving up reliance on foreign
private capital and bringing under the MRPT Act ventures
abroad of Indian capital singly or in combination with western
countries. While conceding that for some time India will
have to export manufactures to Bangla Desh and import raw
materials from that country, he makes it emphatically clear
that there can be no repetition of the pre-partition economic
relationship of complementarity which really meant exploitation with Calcutta as the centre and East Bengal as its hinterland.

Professor Chattopadhyay is, however, all in favour of
mutual cooperation and integrated action for mutual benefit
such as in the development of hydel power, development of
inland waterways, flood control, and the setting up of a jute
community and possibly a tea community as well if Ceylon
is agreeable. He would also favour action in terms of the
FAO study on a perspective plan for the whole of the Lower
Brahmaputra-Ganges basin that includes both Bangla Desh
and neighbouring parts of India. Another suggestion that
he makes is the possibility of launching a movement in Bangla
Desh for the Kibutz type of model villages for cooperative self
management. Professor Chattopadhyay is evidently appre-
hensive of the forces that may prevent the development of
Bangla Desh on socialist lines and would want advance action

taken to counter such forces, including in them action by India herself to refashion her own economy.

I may conclude this introductory analysis by referring to some of my own thoughts on the subject. A part of what I have to say is already to be found in my opening speech to the panel discussion which has been included as an appendix to this volume. I am glad to find broad endorsement of what I then said in the views expressed by the experts who have contributed to this volume. All that I would now like to add is that a bright economic future awaits both Bangla Desh and India, especially its eastern region, if there is mutual understanding, mutual faith, and mutually beneficial but cooperative and integrated action on the part of both the countries. Nature has given a certain identity of interest to the eastern part of the Indian subcontinent, which political boundaries need not prevent full advantage being taken of this identity for the lasting welfare and mutual benefit of the two peoples. Flood control, power development, agricultural growth, use of scientific research and technology, and mutual cooperation in facing problems of foreign trade and foreign aid—all these are areas which offer ample scope for mutual discussion, mutual understanding, and cooperative action. What is important is to see that, from the very beginning, the approach and the relationship should be of that between equals, independent Bengla Desh and independent India, and nothing should be forced directly or indirectly on either party in the relationship. India is not the big brother nor is Bangla Desh the small brother. They are both brothers who have discovered their kinship in shared sacrifice of life and in blood, sweat and tears. Once this is firmly grasped and becomes the base for India-Bangla Desh relationship, I have no doubt whatsoever about the bright prospects that await the economic future of both the countries.

Fortunately, both countries have as their Prime Ministers today persons who enjoy each other's confidence, share the same ideals and values and have shown in action their strong will for intelligent and immediate action. With nature making its contribution, emotion and goodwill its cementing force, intelligent and mutually trustworthy experts their intellectual and analytical assistance, and, above all, with Sheikh Mujibur Rahman as Prime Minister of Bangla Desh and Indira Gandhi as Prime Minister of India, the economic prospects of Bangla Desh are bright indeed and will soon be emerging to make the two countries the lasting bastion of peace and progress on the subcontinent, and, in due course, on this continent of Asia itself.

ARJUN SENGUPTA

REGIONAL DISPARITY AND ECONOMIC DEVELOPMENT OF PAKISTAN*

I

The Facts

WHEN PAKISTAN WAS created in 1947, there was little in the nature of its economy which could have indicated the way its western wing would grow to dominate its eastern part. It was almost completely an agricultural economy, with the East as the world's largest producer of raw jute and the West a major exporter of raw cotton and between them practically self-sufficient in food. There were only 34 factories in the whole of Pakistan with a total employment of about 26,000 persons. Three years after Independence, West Pakistan had only three textile mills, and the East, still producing about 75 per cent of the total world output of jute, had virtually no capacity to produce any jute manufactures. There were just a few plants for sugar refining, tea processing, and manufacture of cement. Virtually all the manufactures used in Pakistan were imported.

---

*Published in *Economic and Political Weekly*, Vol. VI, Nos. 45 and 46, 6 and 13 November 1971.

Nor was it true that natural resources or geographical conditions favoured the western wing more than East Pakistan.
Rapid growth in agriculture would have required large expenditure in any case, but the potential for East Pakistan was
definitely no worse than for West Pakistan. It had a much
larger area of fertile land and plenty of rainfall. To increase
output and productivity, it needed investment in coastal
embankments, flood control measures and low-lift pump
irrigation, and the supply of fertilizers. But that would hardly
cost more than what was required in West Pakistan, given its
relatively barren lands, problems of water-logging and salinity
and the resulting necessity for an expensive network of irrigation canals. Indeed, a recent study has shown that even
tubewells—the one factor that is regarded as the centrepiece
of the agricultural prosperity of West Pakistan—had a very
substantial potential of return in East Pakistan, at a not much
greater cost.[1] They probably could not have been financed
by private farmers as they were in West Pakistan and the
Government might have had to come forward in a much bigger
way. But in terms of social cost, there was nothing in the
nature of the agriculture of East Pakistan that could have made
its potential for growth any lower than that of West Pakistan.
In fact, in a study of 1963, Mahbub-ul Haq, one of the architects
of economic policy under President Ayub, gave an edge to
East Pakistan over the West in the agricultural field, and wrote:
"If proper steps are taken, the eastern wing is destined to
become the granary for the whole of Pakistan."[2]

For the potential growth in industries, both the regions

[1] Ghulam Mohammad, "Development of Irrigated Agriculture in East
Pakistan: Some Basic Considerations", Pakistan Development Review, 1956.
[2] Mahbub-ul Haq, The Strategy of Economic Planning: A Case Study of
Pakistan, 1963.

were on equal footing. Both were poor in industrial raw materials and minerals. Except for raw cotton in the West and raw jute in the East, that allowed a very rapid growth of the respective textiles manufactures, the availability of other agricultural materials was not so large as to permit any significant growth of modern industries. While West Pakistan had some potential for sugar, paper-board and possibly edible oil, East Pakistan had the potential for leather, paper from soft wood, and tea processing. Some tobacco was grown, more in the West than in the East. Mineral resources in Pakistan are not substantial, and most of them have been discovered only in recent periods. Large deposits of natural gas were discovered at Sui in West Pakistan only in 1952 and their productive use started in 1955. Subsequently, several other sites with deposits of gas and small amounts of other minerals were discovered in both the wings of Pakistan. But all these could hardly explain any comparative advantage in industrial growth for West Pakistan.

Not Due to Initial Differences

It is important to emphasize this point to dispel the widely held misconceptions about Pakistan's economic development. Over the years of the history of this country after Independence, its western wing developed much more rapidly than East Pakistan in nearly all the major fields of economic activity. But if one looked into the details of the initial conditions of Pakistan's development, in terms of factor endowments, resource position, or growth potential, one could not seriously maintain that it was in the nature of things that West Pakistan should dominate the East or that a different set of policies could not have achieved quite a different pattern of

regional development. Between 1947 and 1950, the total
regional income of East Pakistan was almost certainly higher
than that of West Pakistan. Availability of power was negligible, and the contribution of transport and communications
to provincial income was somewhat larger in East Pakistan
than in the West. Income generated from services was larger
in West Pakistan but the number of scheduled banks in East
Pakistan was 111 in 1948 as compared with 89 in the West.[3]
West Pakistan had a large irrigation network that was developed
over several decades in the past, but considering the vast
territory of the province and conditions of the soil and the
climate, they were very inadequate to push through a rapid
growth in agriculture. One could not therefore explain the
growth in regional disparity by initial differences in the infrastructure of the two provinces.

It was said above that in the initial years the regional income
in East Pakistan was *almost certainly* higher than that in the
West, for it is very difficult to have a definite picture of the
growth of national income of Pakistan on a regional basis. For
the first time in 1964 official estimates of regional incomes were
given by the CSO and that also only for the years 1959-60 to
1962-63. Khan and Bergan[4] worked on the raw data of CSO
and produced two series of gross provincial product (at 1959-60
factor cost) for the two wings of Pakistan. A summary of
these is given in Table 1. But there are other scholars who
attempted to estimate regional incomes and their disparity.
Their methods of estimation were different both in terms of

---

[3] Quoted by M. Anisur Rahman from *Economic Survey of East Pakistan*,
1968-69.

[4] Khan and Bergan, "Measurement of Structural Change in the Pakistan
Economy: A Review of National Income Estimates", *Pakistan Development
Review*, 1966.

definition, i.e., whether they are gross or net, at factor cost or market prices, etc., and in terms of items included or excluded or how they were allocated to different provinces.

But still the differences in the estimates of regional incomes in the initial period were all in the same direction. For example, Khandkar[5] found for 1950-51 that regional income of East Pakistan was 10 per cent higher than that of West Pakistan. Haq's estimates show higher regional income in East Pakistan in relation to West Pakistan from 1949-50 to 1952-53. In 1951-52, East Pakistan's income was 5 per cent higher and in 1952-53, it was 8 per cent higher than West Pakistan's. Papanek's estimates[6] were for regional GDP at market prices, and in 1949-50 the income of East Pakistan was more than 10 per cent higher than that of West. The regional incomes, according to Papanek, became just about equal in 1954-55.

Khan and Bergan's estimate, as seen in Table 1, also reveals a higher provincial product for East Pakistan than for West in 1949-50. They also show that East Pakistan's income remained higher until 1953-54. From 1954-55, the picture changed and West Pakistan's income exceeded East's for the first time that year, after which the gap continued to widen throughout the period. It will also be seen that in the value added in transport and communication, the share of the two wings was very similar. The value added in electricity, gas, and water in the initial years was very small in both the provinces. Until about 1953-54, West Pakistan's edge over East in trade was very small, hardly exceeding 7 to 8 per cent.

---

[5] R.H. Khandkar, "The Pattern of a Divided Economy: A National Income Analysis of India and Pakistan", *The Journal of Royal Statistical Society*, general series, 1955.

[6] Papanek, *Pakistan's Development*, Harvard, 1967.

TABLE I

GROSS PROVINCIAL PRODUCT OF EAST AND WEST PAKISTAN

(at 1959-60 factor cost, in crores of Rs)

	1949-50		1954-55		1959-60		1963-64	
	East	West	East	West	East	West	East	West
Gross Provincial Product	1237.40	1209.10	1381.60	1410.60	1497.20	1646.70	1867.10	2009.00
of which								
Agriculture	807.40	659.50	870.40	694.80	904.20	771.10	1059.90	875.60
Manufacturing	47.20	96.10	65.10	156.90	91.20	201.80	137.10	269.40
Large scale	(6.90)	(27.70)	(20.00)	(80.20)	(40.60)	(115.90)	(80.90)	(74.10)
Small scale	(40.30)	(68.40)	(45.10)	(76.70)	(50.60)	(85.90)	(56.20)	(95.30)
Construction	5.80	17.90	12.60	28.90	22.40	42.70	67.30	83.70
Electricity, gas, water	0.60	2.70	1.00	3.70	2.00	8.70	9.30	14.20
Transport and communi-cation	63.10	60.80	77.90	81.00	90.00	92.10	112.70	111.80
Trade	137.90	147.70	147.80	177.70	156.00	210.50	208.70	274.60
Population (m)	42.25	35.31	47.70	39.87	53.85	45.03	59.67	49.89
GPP per capita (Rs)	293	342	290	354	278	366	313	403

SOURCE: Khan and Bergan, fn. 4.

Despite the higher regional income of East Pakistan in the initial years, the per capita income of East was lower than that of West from the beginning. This was the conclusion of all the available estimates for regional incomes. Khan and Bergan's estimates show that the per capita GPP of East Pakistan was not only lower than that of West, but was also declining more or less steadily till about 1959-60. This is also corroborated by other available estimates. The extent of disparity, defined as the excess of West Pakistan's per capita income over East's, was of course different for different estimates, since this depended on the differences in the estimates of both gross provincial product and regional population. Khan and Bergan's figures for population are close to the official. They assume equal average annual compound rates of growth of population for both the wings—2.4 per cent for the period 1949-50 to 1959-60, and 2.6 per cent for 1959-60 to 1964-65. These figures follow the estimates of the Planning Commission which adjusted for underenumeration of the figures of 1961 Census according to which the average rate of annual increase was 2.36 per cent for West and 1.91 per cent for East Pakistan. If West Pakistan's population actually grew at a faster rate than East Pakistan's, the per capita disparity figures, computed from Khan and Bergan, would of course be overestimates. But it should be noted that population growth rates have been used for estimating the output of some sectors, e.g. fish in East Pakistan and small-scale industries and services in both the wings. So an overestimate of population would affect both the numerator and the denominator of per capita income figures.

But there are other considerations which suggest that the Khan and Bergan estimates of regional incomes understate the extent of disparity. The CSO estimates of national income provide a regional breakdown of about 97 per cent of total national income. A regional breakdown was not attempted for the remaining 3 per cent of incomes originating in banking and insurance, inter-wing communication and central government and defence activities. Khan and Bergan, working with the CSO data, extended the regional incomes series from 1949-50 to 1963-64, by allocating these incomes to the two wings on a fifty-fifty ratio. This procedure has been challenged by Anisur Rahman[7]. He suggests a regional breakdown of incomes originating in banking and insurance based on the provincial distribution of deposits and advances of scheduled banks which showed a proportion of 73:27 in favour of West Pakistan. And for incomes originating in central government and defence, he suggests an allocation of 74.5:25.5 on the basis of the distribution of the labour force in public administration for the year 1955. S.R. Bose[8] in another context provides an estimate of gross provincial product of East Pakistan by allocating to the East 37 per cent of the value added in transport and communication, 33 per cent of banking and insurance, and 30 per cent of central government defence. Except for these items, for which Khan and Bergan allocate 50 per cent to East Pakistan, Bose's estimates are similar to Khan and Bergan's. The percentages used by Bose, as he mentions, "were estimated by the CSO and used by a group of experts in Transportation Survey of East Pakistan".

The second column of Table 2 has been calculated from

[7] Anisur Rahman, "East-West Pakistan: A Problem of Political Economy of Planning" (mimeographed).

[8] S.R. Bose, "The Trend of Real Income of the Rural Poor", *Pakistan Development Review*, 1968.

Bose's figures for East Pakistan and Khan and Bergan's figures for the whole of Pakistan. It will be seen that these estimates considerably increase, throughout the period, the extent of disparity as measured by the ratio of per capita gross provincial product of West Pakistan to that of East Pakistan. This confirms our statement that Khan and Bergan figures may be regarded as underestimates of the extent of disparity.

Yearly Comparisons Not Valid

Lest one is carried away by these statistics of yearly disparity, I must add that one must not make too much of the absolute figures of gross domestic products, especially their regional breakdown. For many sectors, the estimates are based on assumptions that are subject to unknown errors, the size of which for some years may be quite large. For example, in agriculture, the estimates use a variable called "normal" yields which are based on official crop-cutting experiments of questionable reliability. In West Pakistan, a number of crop-cutting experiments based on probability sampling for wheat and cotton showed that the official figures generally underestimated the yields by 10 to 15 per cent. Official estimates also tend to overstate production in a poor crop year and understate it in a good year. Similarly, a recent CSO study showed that the CMI figures for 1959-60 of the value added in large-scale industry were underestimates to the extent of 9.5 per cent in East Pakistan and 5.8 per cent in West Pakistan.[9]

In such a situation yearly comparisons of per capita GPP may not make much sense. One can place some reliance only on the picture that emerges from the trends over a

[9] See Khan and Bergan (fn. 4) for the details of different sectors.

number of years, hopefully expecting that some of the large errors would be cancelled out. The end year figures of disparity as given in Table 2 up to 1959-60 give a picture that corresponds to the trends fitted to annual figures of disparity between 1949-50 and 1959-60. There is a distinct impression of widening disparity with time, especially during the First Plan period. For the Second Plan period after 1959-60, the end year figures of disparity calculated from Khan and Bergan and estimates based on Bose, as given in Table 2, would suggest that per capita disparity declined from 1959-60 to 1963-64. But the annual figures for these five years do not reveal any trend whatsoever.

Column 3 of Table 2 presents estimates of gross provincial product made by Papanek and the disparity figures calculated from them. The estimates are included for two reasons. First, Papanek's attempts are theoretically much more in conformity with the index of structural change and regional development than the official estimates. Trend figures are used for major crops to reduce random fluctuations, giving typical rather than actual value added in crop production. For manufacturing, Papanek uses the results of a survey conducted by him rather than the CMI figures, which generally give a larger value added and a larger growth rate than survey data. Furthermore, Papanek's figures are in market prices, while the official estimates are at factor cost. With a rapidly increasing amount of indirect taxes accompanying the growth of industry and also agriculture, domestic product at market prices are much better indicators of the physical increase in output than GDP at factor cost. Unfortunately, given the paucity of information, in actual practice the allocation of indirect taxes and subsidies to different sectors is very difficult and

TABLE 2

DISPARITY IN REGIONAL INCOMES

(Gross Provincial Product in crores of rupees and Per Capita GPP in (Rs.)

	Khan and Bergan		Bose*		Papanek**	
	East	West	East	West	East	West
1949—50	1237.40 (293)	1209.10 (342)	1205.20 (285)	1242.10 (352)	1313 (305)	1183 (330)
Disparity	1.17		1.24		1.08	
1954—55	1381.60 (290)	1410.60 (354)	1343.80 (282)	1448.20 (365)	1432 (298)	1431 (356)
Disparity	1.22		1.29		1.19	
1959—60	1497.20 (278)	1646.70 (366)	1456.80 (270)	1687.10 (375)	1559 (288)	1679 (373)
Disparity	1.32		1.39		1.29	
1963—64	1867.10 (313)	2009.00 (403)	1817.10 (304)	2059.10 (413)	1999+ (327)	2379+ (464)
Disparity	1.29		1.36		1.42	

NOTE: Disparity refers to the ratio of per capita GPP of West Pakistan over that of East Pakistan. The estimates of Khan and Bergan and of Bose are at 1959-60 factor cost. Papanek's figures are of gross domestic product at market prices, at constant 1959-60 prices.

Figures in brackets represent per capita GPP.

* Calculated from Bose's figures for East Pakistan GPP.

** Papanek uses trend data for major crops, and a partly arbitrary allocation of indirect taxes and subsidies. He mentions "these data are not reliable".

+ Refers to 1964-65.

SOURCES: Khan and Bergan, fn. 4; Bose, fn. 8, and Papanek, fn. 6.

subject to significant errors.

Secondly, Papanek's estimates show for the initial years, a much larger gross provincial product for East Pakistan than the official estimates. Also Papanek's figures show a widening disparity of the per capita GNP with time, not only up to 1959-60 but also during the Second Plan up to 1964-65, contrary to the estimates based on official figures. In his academic honesty, Papanek observes: "These data are not reliable. By some plausible changes in assumption, East Pakistan's domestic product can be shown to have grown more or less rapidly than West Pakistan's in the 1959-60 to 1960-65 period." In view of the fact that the official estimates are also largely based on guesses and *ad hoc* assumptions, one cannot easily form a judgment about the relative reliability of Papanek's estimates vis-a-vis the official figures. So I have presented in Table 2, Papanek's figures, side by side with the official figures.

No Estimate For Third Plan

For the Third Plan, no estimate of the regional breakdown of the gross national product of Pakistan is available. In Table 3, I have presented some estimates of gross provincial product of East and West Pakistan from secondary sources, but following as far as possible the procedures of Khan and Bergan. A West Pakistan document, published by the Planning and Development Board, Bureau of Statistics, Lahore, called *Performance Statistics of West Pakistan,* April 1969, gives a series of gross provincial (domestic) product of West Pakistan for the period 1964-65 to 1968-69 and of unallocable income between the two wings up to 1967-68, all at constant factor cost of 1959-60. To make it comparable with the

Khan and Bergan procedures, I added the net factor incomes from abroad to the unallocable incomes, and allocated 50 per cent of that to West Pakistan. The total figure for West Pakistan for every year was deducted from the GNP figures at 1959-60 factor cost for the whole of Pakistan as given in *Pakistan Economic Survey 1969-70*, to get the gross provincial product for East Pakistan. For the year 1968-69, for which figures of unallocable income between the two wings is not available—mainly because of no separation between the central public administration and defence and total public administration figures—5 per cent of the total GNP for that year was taken out and 50 per cent of that was allocated to West Pakistan. (The unallocable incomes with the net factor incomes constituted about 5 per cent of the preceding few years.) For the year 1969-70, a clue was taken from the Fourth Plan document (p. 535), stating that provisional estimates for 1969-70 indicate that the gross regional product of East Pakistan has increased only by 22 per cent over the base year figure for the Third Plan. This gave the figure for East Pakistan's GPP for 1969-70 over 1964-65, and West Pakistan's figures were obtained by deducting this from the overall GNP figures. The population estimates are rather rough, taken from the all-Pakistan figures from the Economic Survey and allocating 45 per cent to West Pakistan—following approximately the ratio of the last few years of Khan and Bergan estimates.

Again, one should not attach too much weight to the yearly figures of disparity. But one cannot escape the conclusion that over the years of the Third Plan there was a definite tendency for sharply widening disparity. So, even though during the Second Plan period there was no trend in the figures for disparity—it was neither rising nor falling—during the Third

Plan it was clearly increasing. This is corroborated by other estimates of the rates of growth of gross provincial product. During 1959-60 to 1964-65, the Second Plan period, the GPP of East Pakistan grew at 5.3 per cent a year (compound rate) and that of West Pakistan grew at 5.4 per cent a year.[10] But during the Third Plan, according to Pakistan Economic Survey, 1969-70, the annual average growth rate in East Pakistan was 4.1 per cent as against 6.1 per cent for West Pakistan. Assuming the same growth rate for population of the two regions, as we have done, it is clear that the disparity was widening during the Third Plan.

The measurement of disparity based on a comparison of the per capita gross provincial product at constant factor cost of the two regions—a procedure followed by Khan and Bergan and all others that we have mentioned so far—is open to another more fundamental criticism. The regional GPP's are calculated as quantities multiplied by same base year prices and generally indicate the value of money income in terms of base-year purchasing power of money. But if one rupee in East Pakistan had a purchasing power in the base period different from that in West Pakistan, the ratio of per capita GPP at constant prices of the two regions could not reflect the disparity in terms of per capita real income. Anisur Rahman makes this point forcefully.[11] He quotes from the Second Five-Year Plan (p. 59): "Prices of similar goods have generally been higher in East Pakistan than in West Pakistan, the difference sometimes far exceeding the cost of transport and distribution." An examination of the data would reveal that price differences widened during the Second Plan period and the subsequent

---

[10] Stephen Lewis, *Pakistan: Industrialization and Trade Policies*, p. 139.
[11] Anisur Rahman, *op. cit.* (fn 7).

years, which means that if the base year was chosen from a more recent period, the differences in the purchasing power of money between the two regions would be greater. In such a situation the disparity in the per capita constant price GPP would definitely understate the disparity in real income.

The problem is to find an index which would show the regional income of East Pakistan when the value added in different sectors are calculated at West Pakistan's prices relative to the regional income of West Pakistan calculated at West Pakistan's prices. It is almost certain that this index would have been much lower and hence our measure of disparity (i.e. per capita GPP of West Pakistan/per capita GPP of East Pakistan) is much higher than what is indicated by

TABLE 3

GROSS PROVINCIAL PRODUCT FOR EAST AND WEST PAKISTAN

Estimates for 1964-65 to 1968-69 at 1959-60 Factor Cost

	West Pakistan		East Pakistan		Disparity*
	Total (Rs crores)	Per Capita (Rs)	Total (Rs crores)	Per Capita (Rs)	
1964-65	2244.05	443	1861.75	301	1.47
1965-66	2243.15	459	1953.65	303	1.51
1966-67	2459.60	461	2053.70	315	1.46
1967-68	2708.15	494	2142.95	320	1.54
1968-69**	2891.22	514	2237.48	325	1.58
1969-70**	3156.30	546	2271.33	321	1.70

*Disparity is the ratio of per capita GPP of West Pakistan to that of East Pakistan.

**Rough estimates.

SOURCE: *Pakistan Economic Survey,* 1969-70; Performance Statistics of West Pakistan, April 1969, Government of West Pakistan.

the constant price per capita gross provincial product. Unless one does the full exercise, one cannot really say anything more precise or quantitative than this. But it may be of some interest to note the exercise done by Mahbub ul Haq. He finds that in East Pakistan both rice and wheat were very much more expensive than in West Pakistan, and that in West Pakistan rice was more costly than wheat. He then claims that one ton of rice has the same nutritional value as one ton of wheat, and so they should be treated as similar goods. (Incidentally, that rice and wheat should be treated as the same commodity has been pleaded also by Papanek and Anisur Rahman.) He then values East Pakistan's total rice production at the price of wheat in West Pakistan, and also adjusts the value of rice production in West Pakistan by the same price of wheat. This lowers East Pakistan's regional income very substantially, but West Pakistan's income rather marginally. As a result he finds that in 1959-60, the estimate of disparity becomes double the figure obtained from constant price per capita incomes.

Similar exercise can be done easily for other years also as regional estimates of average prices of rice and wheat are available. The price of rice in East Pakistan is generally double the price of wheat in West Pakistan, and since this commodity has a very large weight in East Pakistan's total income, these exercises would definitely show a drastic fall in East Pakistan's regional incomes. No such attempt is made here as it is not quite legitimate, and it is not even an approximate substitute for the full exercise mentioned above.

There was another consequence of the high price of rice in East Pakistan that should be noted. The cereal food of East Pakistan has always been mostly rice. In 1951-52 per capita consumption of rice was about 14.7 ounces a day while that of wheat was 0.1 ounce and of other cereals, mainly gram, another 0.1 ounce a day. In 1959-60, which was a very good crop year, per capita availability of rice went up to 16 ounces a day, and of wheat to 0.4 ounce. Ten years later, in 1969-70, by the time wheat consumption became fairly widespread, per capita consumption of rice was still about 14.6 ounces a day with wheat consumption about 1.4 ounces a day. In West Pakistan, on the other hand, although wheat was the main cereal, its per capita consumption hovered around 9.5 to 10.5 ounces a day and per capita consumption of rice increased steadily from 0.4 ounce a day in 1951-52 to 1.4 ounces in 1959-60 to about 2.4 ounces in 1969-70. These cereals were supplemented substantially by other items like

TABLE 4

PER CAPITA CONSUMPTION OF SOME COMMODITIES

(per year, in lbs)

	1969-70		1959-60		1951-52	
	East Pakistan	West Pakistan	East Pakistan	West Pakistan	East Pakistan	West Pakistan
(1) Wheat	33.10	231.63	9.10	221.80	2.30	225.80
(2) Rice	334.70	53.93	365.00	38.80	335.30	31.90
(3) Pulses (excluding gram)	6.68	8.08	6.80	4.50	11.40	4.50
(4) Fats and oils	6.44	13.99	—	—	—	—
(5) Milk	21.04	228.12	—	—	—	—
(6) Meat	6.00	7.97	—	—	—	—
(7) Fish	24.60	4.49	9.30	3.50	3.90	2.40
(8) Vegetables	80.75	77.78	—	—	—	—
(9) Refined sugar	5.60	15.89	2.60	6.50	2.70	8.00
(10) Tea	0.23	0.92	0.10	1.00	0.10	0.50
(11) Cotton cloth (yds)	10.86	13.22	3.00	9.00	1.70	1.40

jowar, bajra, maize, barley, and gram. In general, per capita consumption of all cereals was almost stable in both the regions throughout the period but was generally higher in East than in West Pakistan. The result was an overwhelming portion of East Pakistan's per capita income, which was substantially lower than that of West Pakistan, was absorbed in the consumption of cereals which were again relatively more expensive in East than in West. It was natural that per capita absorption of other consumer items would be much smaller in East Pakistan compared to that in West Pakistan. This feature was present throughout the period after independence; and in 1969-70, when per capita income at constant prices was much higher than in 1951-52, per capita consumption in East Pakistan of milk was less than a tenth of that in West, of fats and oils less than a half, of refined sugar about a third, often about a fourth, and of meat about 30 per cent of the per capita consumption in West. In 1951-52, per capita consumption of cloth was slightly higher in East than in West. But in 1969-70 per capita consumption of cotton cloth in East Pakistan was only 10.86 yards compared to 13.22 yards in West Pakistan[12] (see Table 4).

II

Some Hypotheses to Explain Growth of Disparity

The picture that emerges from the analysis given in the earlier part is that, although initially there was nothing much in the economic conditions of Pakistan that was noticeably fav-

---

[12] The figures for 1969-70 are taken from the Fourth Five-Year Plan and for earlier years from S.U. Khan, "A Measure of Economic Growth in East and in West Pakistan", *Pakistan Development Review*, 1961.

ourable to West Pakistan, the gross provincial product of West Pakistan was growing much more rapidly than its population relatively to East Pakistan. As a result, the difference between the per capita income of West and East Pakistan widened over the years, and even in the late 1960s there was no indication of a reversal of that tendency. The figures of per capita consumption of some of the major consumption items in the two regions, as given in Table 4, corroborated this evidence of the increasing disparity of per capita income during the period 1950 to 1970.

For the purpose of isolating the principal factors responsible for the disparity, it is fruitful to divide the whole of Pakistan's experience in economic development into two sub-periods: one up to 1950-60, i.e. the end of the First Five-Year Plan, the other after 1960-61, the years of the Second and Third Five-Year Plans.[13] Such periodization for Pakistan's economic development is a general practice now, mainly to stress that there was a breakthrough in Pakistan's growth process with the beginning of the Second Plan period—which incidentally also happened to be just a couple of years after the installation of the Ayub regime. The period of 1949-50 to 1959-60 was a period of relative stagnation of per capita GNP—a rate of growth of 2.4 per cent in GNP being almost neutralized by a 2.3 per cent growth in population. Khan and Bergan estimates showed a decline of per capita GPP by 1 per cent a year for East Pakistan with a 1.1 per cent increase in that for West Pakistan. In the Second Plan period of 1959-60 to 1964-65, Pakistan's GNP grew at

[13] See T.M. Khan, "Growth of National and Per Capita Income in Pakistan" in the IEA volume, *Economic Development in South Asia*, Macmillan, for the characteristics of these periods.

about 5.5 per cent, which was nearly double the growth rate of the preceding decade. And during the Third Plan, the overall growth rate of GNP was about 5.7 per cent. Throughout the decade of 1959-60 to 1969-70, per capita GPP of both the wings increased noticeably, though, as we have seen, it increased faster in West than in East.

But this discontinuity in growth performance is not the principal reason for this periodization in our present context. For, although the per capita GNP was stagnating during 1949-50 to 1959-60, there was a substantial expansion in the industrial activity in Pakistan. The growth rate figures are not useful here, since with a negligible base they show an exhorbitantly high rate of growth of industries. But there is no doubt that rapid industrialization was going on. For our purpose, these are two main characteristics of this periodization. During the period 1949-50 to 1959-60, the growth of agriculture was small in Pakistan, about 1.3 per cent a year. But since 1959-60, there has been a sharp increase in agricultural output, with a growth rate of 3.4 per cent a year during the Second Plan and of about 4.5 per cent a year during the Third Plan. Secondly, since 1959-60, there has been a sharp rise in foreign assistance inflow into Pakistan. During the whole period, 1950 to 1960, the total foreign assistance, including grants and loans, flowing into Pakistan was about $ 1,862 million. During the Second Plan, 1960-65, alone, this inflow was $ 2,365 million, and in the next five years another $ 2,306 million.

The rate of growth in agriculture was low in both provinces during the first decade; but even then the growth rate in West Pakistan, which was 2 per cent a year, was about four times the growth rate in East Pakistan. This alone should go a long way to explain the widening disparity between East and West Pakistan during this period, especially when one considers that agriculture accounted for about 60 to 70 per cent of the regional product of East Pakistan, compared to about 45 to 51 per cent in West Pakistan. But, in addition, there was an interesting factor about relative price movements which further aggravated the problem for East Pakistan.

At the time of the establishment of Pakistan, most of the consumer goods manufactures absorbed in Pakistan were imported from India—a source that was very quickly closed within a few years, so that all such goods had to be imported from abroad. During the Korean boom, Pakistan's export earnings from raw jute and cotton increased substantially, even though Pakistan did not devalue in 1949 together with India and the UK. But this Korean boom was short lived, and when it collapsed there was a drastic fall in Pakistan's exports. The policy that was followed in response to this was not devaluation, but a severe system of import controls by which imports of consumer manufactures were practically forbidden. Since Pakistan's exports were overwhelmingly agricultural, the result was a sharp fall in the terms of trade for agriculture.

Lewis and Hussain[14] have made a detailed study of this phenomenon and found that, although in the initial years the terms of trade for agriculture fell in both the wings, they fell much more sharply in East Pakistan than in West. The falling terms of trade in agriculture and the rising terms of trade in manufactures have been rationalized later in Pakis-

[14] Lewis and Hussain, *Relative Price Changes and Industrialization in Pakistan*, 1951-64.

tan's economic literature as transfer of resources from a "low" savings sector to a "high" saving sector and has been described by, among others, Lewis as a major contributory factor to Pakistan's industrialization. In the case of East Pakistan, a sharp fall in agriculture's terms of trade took away resources from there which were hardly transferred to industries in that same region. We have, therefore, to explain why the resources from agriculture were not transferred to industries in East Pakistan itself, to which we shall come shortly. In any case, it is clear that a relatively sharper fall in the terms of trade for agriculture in East Pakistan as compared to that in West Pakistan reinforced the effect of the relatively lower growth of agriculture in widening the disparity between the two wings.

From around the mid-1950s, the terms of trade for agriculture started rising in both wings. In West Pakistan, it is explained mostly by the rapid expansion in supply of industrial output in the face of a low rate of growth of agriculture. In East Pakistan, expansion of industrial output could explain this only to a limited extent. The major explanation is provided by a rapid increase in interregional trade, where East Pakistan's imports from the West became increasingly those of manufactures. Items like cotton textiles, manufactured tobacco, rape and mustard seed oil, provisions and oil man's stores, sugar, chemicals and drugs, cement, paper board, boots and shoes, and salt, accounted for between 47 and 50 per cent of total imports of East from West Pakistan, during 1955-56 to 1959-60—but only for about 23 per cent of that in 1948-49. The value of total imports of East from West Pakistan increased by 140 per cent between 1948-49 and 1955-56, and by another 85 per cent between 1955-56 and

1959-60.[15]

All these calculations and transactions were made in terms of domestic prices. But the policies of import control, over-valuation of the currency and discrimination against primary exports in the 1950s had differential effects on the relative prices in the two wings. Lewis, in another recent study, has calculated "the ratio of the terms of trade each province's agricultural sector received relative to what it might have received in world trade for the period 1951-52 to 1963-64." He finds that "not only did East Pakistan farmers receive lower prices for their products than did West Pakistan farmers, but they also paid higher prices for their manufactured goods."[16] This is, of course, a notional problem, but it makes clear that the effect of import controls was felt more strongly in East Pakistan, where the agricultural sector was squeezed much more than in West Pakistan.

It should be noted that, although East Pakistan's agriculture was relatively more squeezed than West Pakistan's, it does not follow that the actual amount of transfer of resources from agriculture to industry was greater in East than in West. The value of that amount depends on the portion of the output marketed, and since West Pakistan's agriculture was more commercialized than East Pakistan's, it was quite possible that the amount of transfer of resources from agriculture to industry was larger in West than in East. Lewis thinks this was so, saying that in the mid-1950s, per year, West Pakistan's farmers marketed about $ 500 million of agricultural goods against $ 200 million worth of manufacture resulting in $ 300

[15] Nurul Islam, "Some Aspects of Inter-Wing Trade and Terms of Trade in Pakistan", *Pakistan Development Review*, 1963.

[16] S. Lewis, *op. cit.* (fn. 10), p. 148.

million transfer, while East Pakistan farms marketed $ 300 millions of goods against $ 100 million worth of manufactures, having $ 200 million of transfer of resources from agriculture to industry. The evidence here is scanty but, if it is true, this would be a partial explanation of slow growth of industry in East Pakistan, even if all the resources transferred from agriculture in that province were invested within itself.

TABLE 5

REGIONAL VALUE ADDED IN LARGE-SCALE INDUSTRY AT CONSTANT PRICE 1959-60

(*Rs. crores*)

Year	West	East
1947-48	10	7
1948-49	14	8
1949-50	18	12
1950-51	24	16
1951-52	35	18
1952-53	46	20
1953-54	56	25
1954-55	79	31
1955-56	93	35
1956-57	102	40
1957-58	116	43
1958-59	130	52

NOTES: (1) Large-scale firm: CSO definition—a unit using power employing more than 30 workers any day in the year.

(2) From 1947-1959: Value added by firms with assets of less than Rs 1 million increased only 15 times, while that added by larger firms increased 15 times.

(3) Deflated by regional wholesale prices index of manufactures. In 1951-52, index for East Pakistan was 98.9, for West Pakistan 90.6. This was applied to 1947-51 years for which no index is available.

SOURCE: G.F. Papanek, "Industrial Production and Investment in Pakistan", *Pakistan Development Review*, 1964.

The pattern of industrial development in the two regions is much more complex. In Table 5, we have presented the estimates of value added in large-scale industry in the two wings of Pakistan taken from Papanek's survey data, and it clearly reveals a much higher rate of growth in West Pakistan than in East Pakistan. In the first few years, the rate of growth of industries was very high in both regions as it started from a low base-consumer goods having expanded at the highest rate—and, except for tea and some matches, most of the industries like sugar, elible oil, tobacco and cotton textiles came up in West Pakistan. Intermediate and investment goods industries also expanded at a rapid rate during this period and in the period 1954-55 to 1959-60, their growth rates were almost 70 per cent higher than those of consumer goods industries. A large number of different kinds of industries turned up and, except for jute and paper products, most of these intermediate goods industries were established in West Pakistan.

Table 6 presents a picture of the pattern of industrial activity around the end of our first sub-period of 1949-50 to 1959-60. The census of manufacturing industry of 1957 showed that East Pakistan shared only 18 per cent of the total number of establishments, 30 per cent of their average daily employment and 26 per cent of their gross output. Except for the jute industry—which was entirely in East Pakistan—and paper, the overwhelming part of the output of most other industries originated in West Bengal. Three other industries, which had high growth rates, were sugar, edible oils, and tobacco manufactures of cigaretts. The share of East Pakistan in the physical output of these industries in 1959-60 were 35 per cent, 6 per cent, and 11 per cent respectively.

It will also be seen from this table that most of the industries in the intermediate and investment goods sector—such
as chemicls, basic metals, machinery, electric machinery,
transport equipment, metal products—which showed high
rates of growth in 1954-55 to 1959-60, and had a negligible
share of production in East Pakistan, were heavily dependent
on imported raw materials.

It is interesting to note this as it reveals the importance
of availability of imports in influencing the pattern of industrial development in Pakistan. Capital goods for most of
the industries had to be imported anyway, and, assuming
that they could be availed of in either wing, the location
of the industries would have depended very much on the
availability of raw materials. Location of industries heavily
dependent on imported materials would have been neutral
as between the two wings but for the import policy and the
licensing policy of government and the facilities of social
overhead services. Industries dependent on domestically
produced materials—like cotton textiles, sugar, edible oil,
food, tobacco, footwear, jute textile, tea, and paper—would be
expected to be established in the regions of the supply of
raw materials. But here, also, the availability of imports and
public policy, together with the availability of social overhead
services, played some role in the location and rate of expansion
of these industries, because their plants had to be imported.
There is also evidence that several of these industries would
have been as efficient in East as they were in West Pakistan,
had they been operated in East Pakistan with materials imported from West.

The greater availability of imports in West Pakistan than
in East Pakistan and the related question of transfer of

resources from East to West Pakistan through foreign trade are well-known facts, which are most frequently discussed in the literature on Pakistan's economic development. We do not have to deal with this problem in great detail; presenting of some bare facts should be sufficient. The average annual imports of West Pakistan from abroad during the period 1950-51 to 1954-55 were about Rs 105.31 crores, and during

TABLE 6

SOME ASPECTS OF THE INDUSTRIAL ACTIVITY IN PAKISTAN

Industry	Percentage of total establishments in East Pakistan, 1957	Percentage of total gross output originating in East Pakistan, 1957	Percentage of imported raw materials to total raw materials, 1960	Rate of growth of gross value of output, 1954-55 to 1959-60
Basic metals	4	2	69.8	14.8
Electric machinery	6	2	64.4	40.0
Other machinery	8	5	56.1	33.0
Footwear, etc.	7	4	neg.	12.2
Non-metallic minerals	15	13	15.4	19.8
Rubber products	12	15	na	13.6
Metal products	15	21	75.4	23.0
Transport equipment	16	na	86.1	45.0
Tobacco manufactures	18	na	8.7	18.2
Cotton textiles	11	24	12.3	17.7
Chemicals and chemical products	20	26	61.7	30.0
Printing and publishing	34	19	28.1	11.3
Beverages	29	20		0.6
Food	40	23	4.0	27.0
Leather and leather product.	43	37	18.3	35.0
Paper and paper products	50	89	28.3	22.0

SOURCES: N. Islam, "Some Aspects of Inter-wing Trade and Terms of Trade in Pakistan", *Pakistan Development Review*, 1963; S. Lewis, *Economic Policy and Industrial Growth in Pakistan*, p. 114.

1955-56 to 1959-60, Rs 152.5 crores. The corresponding figures for East Pakistan were 43.94 crores and Rs 62.48 crores, respectively; East Pakistan had a surplus on foreign trade account, of Rs 42.4 crores a year, during the pre-Plan period, and of Rs 35.5 crores per annum during the First Plan period; at the same time it had a deficit in inter-wing trade with West Pakistan throughout the period. Still on the combined balance of trade, including both foreign and inter-wing trade, East Pakistan had a total surplus for 1950-51 to 1959-60, of about Rs 166.6 crores. West Pakistan, on the other hand, had a total deficit on foreign trade account of about Rs 554.5 crores for this whole period. It had a surplus on account of the inter-wing trade of Rs 229.9 crores, but in the combined trade account during this whole period it had a total deficit of Rs 331.6 crores.

Two things emerge from all this. Throughout 1950-51 to 1959-60, there was a net outflow of resources from East Pakistan. It was exporting abroad much more than it was importing, and although in its trade with West Pakistan it was getting more than it paid, the deficit was not sufficient to compensate it for the loss of its resources through foreign trade. West Pakistan was selling more to East Pakistan than it was buying, but it was importing so much more than it was exporting abroad that there was a substantial net inflow of resources to West Pakistan. This net inflow was financed to the extent of 50 per cent by the surplus of trade accounts in East Pakistan. The mechanism was simply that the exporters of East Pakistan surrendered whatever foreign exchange they received to the central bank in exchange of rupees and this foreign exchange they earned was spent largely by importers of West Pakistan. The remaining part of West Pakistan's net deficit on trade account was financed by foreign aid and loans.

Secondly, although during the pre-Plan period there was a foreign assistance inflow of $74.4 million a year, and during the First Plan period, of $198 million a year, throughout this period there was no net inflow of aid to East Pakistan. A net inflow of aid is always reflected in an equivalent deficit on trade account and the trade surplus of East Pakistan reveals that, even if some actual disbursement of foreign aid resources was made, the disbursement was more than matched by the outflow of resources through exports.

By bringing in the questions, such as the foreign exchange rate, one could show that the resource transfers from East Pakistan were even larger. For instance, since Pakistan's currency was very much overvalued during this period, the value of trade surplus in foreign exchange from East Pakistan should have a much higher value in terms of domestic resources than the nominal value in terms of the official exchange rate. The deficit in inter-wing trade account taking place in Pakistan currency should be deducted from a much larger total of surplus on foreign trade account, which would give a correspondingly higher figure for the net resource transfer. Theoretically, this point is correct; but a quantitative measure of this enlarged transfer cannot be given unless one finds out the shadow rate of exchange which would depend on the actual use of foreign exchange in all the different activities. With some foreign aid funds actually flowing in, the problem is even more difficult; for, one dollar of foreign aid may have a quite different shadow value from another dollar of foreign aid, depending upon the source of aid and the nature of the tying in of such aid.

In any case, it is clear that a substantial part of the resources generated in East Pakistan during this period, which could have been used within that province, were transferred to West Pakistan to finance a large fraction of the total absorption of resources in West Pakistan over and above what was generated in that region. This definitely contributed to the expansion of West Pakistan's economy at a higher rate than that of East Pakistan. But still, it does not explain our problem of growing disparity; for, the question remains: Why was it that a much larger import surplus could be generated in West Pakistan but not in East Pakistan?

A similar point can be raised about the volume of private investment in the two wings. Estimates of private investment are difficult to get—particularly as a time series with a regional breakdown for the period before 1959-60. Mahbub-ul Haq estimates a series on the basis of the use of inputs, and this is probably the most reliable of the generally unreliable estimates and information on this point[17], and can be used to indicate the broad order of magnitudes. Haq shows that, in 1949-50, total private investment in East Pakistan was about Rs 14 crores, while that in West Pakistan was about Rs 38 crores. In 1954-55, the corresponding figures were Rs 20 crores and Rs 55 crores, and in 1959-60, they were Rs 37 crores and Rs 77 crores. These estimates were in current prices, and show that, even in 1959-60, private investment in East Pakistan was less than in West Pakistan a decade earlier in 1949-50. Total private investment in West Pakistan, throughout the period, was about 2 to 2.7 times that in East Pakistan. If these figures are roughly representative of what

[17] Mahbub-ul Haq, *op. cit.* (fn. 2).

actually happened, then they, together with regional distribution of public investment, should go a long way to explain the higher growth in West Pakistan than in East Pakistan. But it still begs the question: Why did private investment flow so much to West Pakistan and not to East Pakistan? In other words, why was it more profitable to invest in West rather than in East Pakistan.

This leads us to examine in greater detail the nature of government policy in Pakistan—first, in terms of public expenditure, and then, in terms of import policy. It should be noted at the beginning that, although public development expenditure in Pakistan was quite substantial, its main aim was to aid the private sector in its process of development. During the pre-Plan period, i.e. between 1948-49 and 1954-55, public development expenditure was about Rs 50 crores per year, and over 80 per cent of that went to West Pakistan.[18] A six-year Development Programme was adopted in 1950, under which about Rs 250 crores were spent up to 1954, mostly on the development of the infrastructure facilities. In 1952 was established the Pakistan Industrial Development Corporation (PIDC) which was supposed to develop industries, with or without private participation, in areas where private investment was not forthcoming. Its head office was located in Karachi, and it was immensely successful in promoting industrial development in West Pakistan through its pioneering activities and diversification of industries among various lines of consumer and intermediate goods—such as woollens, sugar, fruit canning, chemicals, telephones, cement, fertilizer, and

---

[18] Most of the figures relating to public development expenditures are taken from Aklaqur Rahman, "The Role of the Public Sector in the Economic Development of Pakistan", in the IEA volume, *op. cit.*

so on. PIDC also initiated the exploitation of the reserves
of natural gas at Sui. Some attempt was made to start jute
and other manufacturing by PIDC in East Pakistan, but
this was far less than was required to generate a momentum.
Besides, little was done to develop infrastructural facilities.

The formulation of the First Plan, 1955-56 to 1959-60,
it is generally accepted, was guided mostly by the structural
changes that had accrued in West Pakistan in the pre-Plan
period. About Rs 400 crores of public development expenditure during this plan went to West Pakistan compared to only
Rs 113 crores to East Pakistan. The overwhelming part of
this expenditure in both the wings went to water, power,
transport, and communications. The absolute amount, of
Rs 187 crores, going to these two sectors in West Pakistan,
was about three times the amount of Rs 64 crores that went to
East Pakistan for the same two sectors. The amount for
agriculture was Rs 34.9 crores in West Pakistan compared to
Rs 22.1 crores in East Pakistan. But manufacturing and
mining absorbed about Rs 75 crores in West Pakistan, as
against only Rs 3.3 crores in East Pakistan.

It is not easy to appreciate the reasons why planned public
development expenditures were so much lower in East Pakistan than it was in West Pakistan. Even during the Second
Plan, only about Rs 631 crores of public development expenditure went to East Pakistan, compared to Rs 763 crores
to West Pakistan. It is not true that the problem of disparity
went unnoticed in official circles. The first Plan document
states (p.74): "The problem of regional development is specially acute between East and West Pakistan. Because they
are more than a thousand miles apart, there is very little
movement of population between the two wings. Even

the movements of goods cannot be as free and smooth as in contiguous areas. This means that, so far as possible, and subject to other objectives of the programme, economic opportunities should be moved to the people, rather than people to the opportunities." Yet the plan allocations and their implementation do not reveal any attempt to follow this dictum in practice.

Was it that the planners thought that the potential for growth was much lower in East than in West Pakistan? The First Plan (p. 75) stated that there was not "any significant difference in the magnitude of potential economic opportunities between the two wings." But in the Second Plan, the lower allocation to East Pakistan was justified by stating that the regional allocations were guided by the need to "maximize development in the less developed parts of the country without prejudicing national development as a whole" (p. 398). The implicit assumptions were, of course, not made clear as to why there should be this conflict between the growth of East Pakistan and the overall growth of the country.

In any case, the major impact of public development expenditure was a rapid development of infrastructural facilities. The way these were differentially developed in the two regions during 1949-50 to 1959-60 was definitely responsible for any substantial difference in the productivity of investment which was implicitly referred to in the Second Plan. The rate of installing generating capacity during 1947-60 was about 16 per cent a year. The net availability of electricity in East Pakistan in 1951-52 was 20,225 thousand Kwh and in 1955-56, 43,969 thousand Kwh, while in 1959-60 it went up to 77,226 thousand Kwh. The corresponding figures for West Pakistan were 295,474 thousand Kwh, 705,982 thousand Kwh and 1,198,779 thousand Kwh. In 1959-60, the figures for the numbers per million persons of railway wagons were 6 for East Pakistan and 166 for West; of buses and trucks, 85 in East and 495 in West; of post offices, 83 in East, 186 in West; miles of high-type roads per million persons was 28 for East and 225 for West; and the number of branch offices of banks was 110 in East compared to 286 in West.[19] Such a public development expenditure policy created social overhead facilities much more rapidly in West Pakistan than in East, and consequently had an external economic effect of stimulating private investment through increased profitability.

The exchange control policy, on the other hand, created a mechanism which effectively allocated much of the total import capacity, i.e. export earnings plus foreign aid, in favour of West Pakistan. In the beginning of the period, when Pakistan had to depend on foreign trade for most of the commodities supplied at home, a policy of open general licensing was followed, according to which those who had the capacity and resources to import could become importers. It is at this time that the trading activities of Pakistan were virtually monopolized by a few trading groups—mostly immigrants from India and operating in and around Karachi. They already had long experience in trading with a well-developed nexus of communications and organization, and they had substantial resources in the form of liquid capital.[20]

With the collapse of the Korean boom, Pakistan Government introduced stringent quantitative controls on imports; and

---

[19] Mahbub-ul Haq, *op. cit.* (fn. 2), p. 109.

[20] For the details about growth and antecedents of the traders, see Papanek, *op. cit.* (fn. 6).

from 1953 to 1959, about all imports into Pakistan came
under one or other form of import licences which regulated
imports both by type and value of commodities as well as by
destination to specific regions. The predominant licences
were commercial and industrial licences. Commercial licences
allowed imports of commodities that could be resold, and were
highly profitable as the prices they fetched in the domestic markets were well above the c.i.f. prices with duties. The allocation of these licences and amounts of imports of each commodity
were determined by the amounts the licence-holders had
actually imported during 1950-52. Industrial licences, on
the other hand, allowed the manufacturers to import specific
quotas of machinery and equipment, spare parts, and raw
materials, for their own use; and these were legally non-
saleable. Quotas were fixed in terms of installed capacities
and once an investment was sanctioned and capacity was
installed, quota holders became regularly entitled to imports
in the following years.

Both these licences—which accounted for about two-thirds
of all imports to the private sector throughout 1950 to 1964—
favoured the trading communities in Karachi. Because they
were predominant importers during 1950-52, they got most
of the share of commercial imports, and enormous profits as
windfall gains during the period of stringent restrictions on
imports. The overwhelming portion of these commercial licences—between one-half and two-thirds—were used to import
raw materials.[21] Naqvi has shown that, in 1959, 95 per cent

[21] For figures and analysis of licensing policies, see Naqvi, "The Allocation
Biases of Pakistan's Commercial Policy", *Pakistan Development Review*, 1966;
and Thomas, "Import Licensing and Import Liberalization in Pakistan",
Pakistan Development Review, 1966.

of raw materials for capital goods and 44 per cent of raw materials for consumer goods were imported under commercial licensing.

Imports of raw materials were highly profitable, because alongside the strict control on final consumer goods imports the rapid expansion of highly profitable consumer goods industries essentially depended on raw materials. Further although capital goods imports were more freely allowed, as we have already noted above, industries in this sector expanded at a very rapid rate raising the profitability on the raw materials for capital goods.

This also suggests that, for traders who were importing raw materials, it would be increasingly attractive to move into direct production of final goods. Indeed, although profits earned on trading activities were large, since the accounting units of imports were more or less fixed, there was little scope for further expansion of these activities; compared to that, investment in industrial activities become highly profitable. Papanek talks about a 50 to 100 per cent profit in the initial years. While these figures may not be reliable, there is evidence provided by Papanek that industrial investment was about 30 per cent more profitable during 1947-55 than in 1956-58. So the traders with capital resources could enter the industrial field and reap the advantage of the profitabilities of the initial years.

Papanek provides figures to show how the traders, who converted themselves into industrialists, came to dominate the field of industrial investment and activities during this period. For our present purpose, what is relevant is, first, that by becoming industrialists the groups which controlled the commercial licences, also tended to dominate industrial licences; secondly, that since they were traders operating mostly in and around Karachi, there was a built-in bias in their activities in favour of Karachi and of West Pakistan—a bias which was also reinforced by the excellent social overhead facilities of that city which even before Partition was one of the most modern port-cities in the subcontinent. Further, since Karachi was also the capital, the rate of development of overhead facilities was high and the sanctions for industrial investment there were much easier to obtain. The result was a quite phenomenal increase in industrial activity in Karachi during this period. In 1954, of the total value added in large-scale manufacturing in Pakistan, Rs 68.8 crores, 31 per cent was in Karachi as against 49 per cent in the rest of West Pakistan, and only 20 per cent in East Pakistan. The corresponding figures for 1959-60 were 30 per cent in Karachi, 45 per cent in the rest of West Pakistan, and only 25 per cent in East Pakistan —cut of a total of about Rs 155 crores.

Thus, the factors that tilted the balance of supply of imports to West Pakistan were as follows:

(a) The traders, who dominated the field of private imports, belonged to West Pakistan and particularly to Karachi and they had their trade connections and organizational channels developed mostly in West Pakistan. Their operation in East Pakistan would have to be attracted by considerably higher profit margin to compensate for their breaking into new lines of venture.

(b) As the traders themselves become industrialists or closely associated with them, and as these industries cropped up mostly in West Pakistan and particularly Karachi, the availability of imports tended to get concentrated in West Pakistan.

(*c*) Industries developed in the Western region because of (*i*) profitability of particular lines of activity, (*ii*) enormous expenditure on and development of social overhead facilities by the government, and (*iii*) the availability of imports through established traders.

The factors (*b*) and (*c*) are interrelated. The most profitable line of activity during the early period was cotton textiles, which accounted for more than a third of all value added by industry in 1958. Papanek has shown that, until 1954, there was a large excess demand for cotton textiles and prices charged were "what the traffic would bear". During 1951-54, whole-sale cloth prices rose by 20 to 30 per cent, while the general wholesale price index fell sharply by about 30 per cent. Raw cotton prices also declined by one-third. All this would indicate high profitability in this line of activity.

The result was that, of the total imports channelled by commercial and industrial licences a much smaller fraction went to East Pakistan. In 1959-60, East Pakistan received 36 per cent of commercial licence imports and about 35 per cent of industrial licence imports, while Karachi alone received 45 per cent of the former and 37 per cent of the latter, and the rest of West Pakistan received only 19 per cent and 28 per cent, respectively.

It is interesting that the regional distribution of government imports followed almost the same pattern as that of private imports. In the pre-Plan period, government imports were less than one-fifth of total imports but in the First Plan period, they amounted to almost one-half; so a deliberate policy on government account imports could go a long way to compensate for market-guided private imports biased in favour of West Pakistan. But during the pre-Plan period East

Pakistan's share in government imports was only 30 per cent and during the First Plan, only about 36 per cent.

The growth of disparity in our second sub-period, between 1959-60 and 1969-70, is much easier to explain. By 1959-60, a whole decade of development and policy led to the building of capacities and assets, trade and production organizations, and social overhead facilities, decisively in favour of West Pakistan. So any additional rupee of investment would be attracted more to West Pakistan than to East. If matters were left entirely to market forces, the disparity would have widened far more sharply than it did during the Second Plan period of 1960-65. There was a sharp rise in public expenditure during this period—almost six times as much as in the First Plan. Although the total of Rs 631 crores was still about 18 per cent lower than public development expenditure in West Pakistan, the step-up was quite substantial for East Pakistan. Expenditure and water and power increased almost four time and that in transport and communications rose more than five times. Expenditure in agriculture was almost the same as in West Pakistan, but in manufacturing and mining it was about 33 per cent higher. Obviously, this was not sufficient to reverse the trend in disparity; in fact, private investment at the end of the Second Plan in East Pakistan was only 20 to 30 per cent of that in West Pakistan. But still, for the first time, a substantial boost was given to the per capita GPP of East Pakistan.

The relevance of the sharp rise in foreign aid during this period—which we chose as a criterion for dividing the sub-periods—should become clear at this point. During the Second Plan, there was a marked fall in the export surplus of East Pakistan indicating a sharp rise in the imports to that region. The annual average of imports rose to Rs 122 crores

during the Second Plan compared to Rs 62.5 crores in the
First Plan. At the same time, West Pakistan's import surplus
increased significantly from Rs 91 crores annually during the
First Plan to Rs 191.5 crores during the Second Plan. Obviously, the transfer of resources from East Pakistan could not
contribute much to finance this import surplus of West
Pakistan. So, this sharp rise in imports of East Pakistan simultaneously with continued increase in the import surplus in
West Pakistan was possible only because of a large increase
in foreign aid inflow.

This increase in foreign aid also enabled the government to
start liberalizing the imports. In 1960, open general licensing
was reintroduced to promote the entry of newcomers to import
trade, and this helped very much the entrepreneur in East
Pakistan. Bonus voucher imports started rising from 1959-60,
and in 1969 the Free List was introduced with a total of 51
items.

The point to note is that, when the availability of foreign
exchange as well as the command over resources that planners
could distribute between the regions increased, the government
chose not to force the diversion of resources to East Pakistan
but to liberalize control and rely more on market incentives.
But, as we have seen, the market was already biased against
East Pakistan. Besides the already installed overhead facilities
and other factors in West Pakistan which made investment
relatively more profitable in this wing, the very fact that this
province was growing at a faster rate reinforced its growth.
Lewis made some calculations to determine the source of
growth in manufacturing industries and found that, in 1959-60
to 1963-64, about 87 per cent of growth in the value added in
manufacturing was explained by the growth of domestic de-

mand as against only 2 per cent from import substitution. In fact, he showed that, over time since the First Plan period, the growth of domestic demand was increasing in importance as a source of growth of manufacturing.

It was only in the Third Plan that public expenditure in East Pakistan exceeded that in West Pakistan. East Pakistan should have got 53 per cent of the target expenditure total of Rs 3,000 crores. This proportion was more or less achieved, but the actual total expenditure was only Rs 2,186 crores—27 per cent less than the target.[22]

As one would have expected, however, given the circumstances, actual private investment was totally different from what was expected. The target of private expenditure during the Third Plan was Rs 2,200 crores, expected to be equally distributed between the two provinces. The realized private investment in East Pakistan was about Rs 544.3 crores which was about one-third of Rs 1,620.3 crores invested in West Pakistan. It is clear that the market still favoured West Pakistan.

[22] All public development expenditure figures exclude large expenditures on the Indus-Basin Replacement works, which were regarded as outside the Plan.

P.C. VERMA

ECONOMIC STAGNATION OF BANGLA DESH

DURING THE LAST 24 years, while Bangla Desh was a part of Pakistan, its economy stagnated. The economic policy pursued by the Central Government of Pakistan forced Bangla Desh to remain economically backward. An analysis of the manner in which economic policy of the Central Government of Pakistan was pursued may be necessary to assess the prospects for the future development of now independent Bangla Desh.

When Pakistan was created, both the regions, West and East, were economically backward. Subsequently, however, while the economy of West Pakistan rapidly developed, the economy of Bangla Desh lagged. Over the entire period of two decades, 1949-50 to 1969-70, the per capita income of Bangla Desh could increase at an annual rate of hardly 0.7 per cent. In fact during the fifties, the per capita income of Bangla Desh declined at an annual rate of 0.3 per cent. On the other hand, over the two decades, the per capita income of West Pakistan increased at an annual rate of 2 per cent. In 1969-70, while per capita income of Bangla Desh was Rs 339 only, the per capita income of West Pakistan was as large as Rs 500. The per capita income of Bangla Desh thus lagged behind that of West Pakistan by Rs 161, that is by 33 per cent.

The structure of Bangla Desh economy also remained backward. The agricultural sector continued to dominate the economy. Even by 1964-65, the share of agricultural sector in gross domestic product was as large as 58 per cent compared to 40 per cent only in West Pakistan. The industrial sector failed to expand to any significant extent in the economy. The share of industrial sector comprising manufacturing and construction was 12 per cent only in Bangla Desh. On the other hand, the share of the industrial sector in West Pakistan was as large as 20 per cent. The manufacturing sector, the crucial sector in industrialization, remained insignificant in Bangla Desh. The share of the manufacturing sector in gross domestic product was 7 per cent only in Bangla Desh compared to more than 14 per cent in West Pakistan. Within the manufacturing sector, the large scale manufacturing sector contributed only 5 per cent to gross domestic product of Bangla Desh compared to 9 per cent in West Pakistan.

The levels of consumption also remained low, in Bangla Desh. Per capita consumption of milk, fats and oils was extremely low. Even by 1969-70, the per capita consumption of milk was 21.04 lbs, of fats and oils 6.44 lbs, and of sugar 5.60 lbs which were hardly 10 per cent, 45 per cent and 35 per cent, respectively, of the corresponding consumption levels in West Pakistan. The consumption level of cotton-cloth was also low. In 1969-70, the per capita consumption of cotton-cloth in Bangla Desh was 10.86 yds which was 20 per cent lower than the corresponding consumption level in West Pakistan.

The policies of the Central Government of Pakistan with regard to developmental expenditure, foreign trade, inter-regional trade and foreign aid worked adversely against

Bangla Desh. The developmental expenditure, which determined generation of production capacities, was extremely limited here. Consequently, Bangla Desh failed to have adequate expansion of production capacities within its economy. During the entire period of two decades, 1950-51 to 1969-70, the developmental expenditure, of both public and private sectors, was Rs 31,303 million only as compared to Rs 62,813 million in West Pakistan. The developmental expenditure in Bangla Desh was hardly 50 per cent of that in West Pakistan.

The small size of developmental expenditure in Bangla Desh was caused by both public and private sectors. The private sector developmental expenditure, during the entire period of two decades, 1950-51 to 1969-70, was Rs 10,934 million only in Bangla Desh compared to Rs 31,986 million in West Pakistan. The private sector developmental expenditure in Bangla Desh was hardly one-third of that in West Pakistan. The small size of private sector developmental expenditure in Bangla Desh was because of the absence of physical infrastructure and other facilities. In fact, during the first decade, 1950-51 to 1959-60, even the whole of domestic savings of Bangla Desh economy were not invested within the economy. During this period, while total gross savings were Rs 8,240 million, the gross investment was Rs 6,720 million only.

The public sector failed to assume a leading role in Bangla Desh which therefore failed to stimulate private sector also. During the period 1950-51 to 1969-70, the public sector developmental expenditure was Rs 20,369 million only in Bangla Desh compared to Rs 30,827 million in West Pakistan. The public sector developmental expenditure in Bangla

Desh was lower by 34 per cent of that in West Pakistan. In fact at per capita level, the discrimination against Bangla Desh was severe. The per capita public sector developmental expenditure of Bangla Desh was hardly 50 per cent of that of West Pakistan.

The public sector developmental expenditure comprised Provincial Government and Central Government expenditures. The smaller size of public sector developmental expenditure in Bangla Desh was caused by severe regional discrimination in Central Government expenditure. At the Provincial Government level of expenditure there was not much difference. During the period, 1950-51 to 1967-68, the development expenditure of Provincial Government was Rs 12,006 million in Bangla Desh and Rs 13,675 million in West Pakistan. However, the Central Government development expenditure, during the same period, was Rs 3,440 million only in Bangla Desh compared to Rs 12,118 million in West Pakistan. The Central Government expenditure in Bangla Desh was less than one third of that in West Pakistan.

In Bangla Desh, the public sector developmental expenditure on physical infrastructure was neglected. During almost the three plan periods, from 1955-56 to 1967-68, the public sector development expenditure on physical infrastructure was Rs 6,579 million only in Bangla Desh compared to Rs 15,744 million in West Pakistan. The public sector developmental expenditure failed to adequately expand physical infrastructure facilities in Bangla Desh. The generation of power, which was necessary for the expansion in various sectors, remained severely inadequate. By 1969-70, the production of electricity in Bangla Desh was of the order of 1,300 million Kwh. In West Pakistan, on the other hand, the production of electricity was of the order of 6,700 million Kwh. The production of electricity in Bangla Desh was hardly one-fifth of that in West Pakistan.

The direct financial assistance to private sector in Bangla Desh was inadequate. The centrally sponsored financial corporations—Industrial Credit and Investment Corporation, Industrial Development Bank, Agricultural Development Bank, and House and Building Finance Corporation—pursued regional discrimination in financial allocations. During the entire period of 1950-51 to 1969-70, the financial assistance of centrally sponsored financial corporations was Rs 2,451.7 million in Bangla Desh compared to 3,793.7 million in West Pakistan. The financial assistance to private sector in Bangla Desh was smaller by 34 per cent of that given to private sector in West Pakistan.

The economy of Bangla Desh was exploited through the mechanism of foreign trade. Bangla Desh always exported more than West Pakistan did. Jute was the principal commodity of export apart from other commodities. During the entire period 1950-51 to 1969-70, the exports of Bangla Desh amounted to Rs 23,303 million whereas the exports of West Pakistan were to the tune of Rs 19,476 million only. Consequently, exports of Bangla Desh exceeded that of West Pakistan by Rs 3,827 million. Although Bangla Desh provided larger export earnings, the Central Government discriminated against Bangla Desh in import allocations. The instrument of import licence was utilized for this purpose. The exporters of Bangla Desh, who deposited foreign exchange, were given rupees. The foreign exchange was sanctioned, however, mostly to importers of West Pakistan. During the entire period 1950-51 to 1969-70, while imports of Bangla Desh were around Rs 19,261 million, the imports of West Pakistan were as large as Rs 41,918 million. The imports of Bangla Desh were lower by Rs 22,657 million, or by 54 per cent of the imports of West Pakistan. The smaller allocations of imports in Bangla Desh prevented expansion and establishment of projects in both the public and private sectors. Foreign complimentory resources could not be adequately imported. The discrimination with this regard was more rigidly followed in the import of capital goods. During the period, 1951-52 to 1964-65, the imports of capital goods including raw material for such production were of Rs 5426.5 million only in Bangla Desh compared to that of Rs 13,088.6 million in West Pakistan. The imports of capital goods in Bangla Desh were hardly 41 per cent of the imports of such goods in West Pakistan.

Inter-regional trade was also utilized for exploiting the economy of Bangla Desh. West Pakistan imported raw materials and certain goods which were not available within her economy from Bangla Desh. The raw materials such as wood and timbers were imported apart from such primary products as betelnuts, spices and others. West Pakistan also imported such commodities as tea, jute goods, paper and paper boards, and matches, to meet their requirements. The total imports of West Pakistan from Bangla Desh during the period 1950-51 to 1969-70 were of Rs 13,180 million. Apart from draining away, the raw material and other commodities, West Pakistan adopted the strategy of supporting her own industries by exporting goods to Bangla Desh market. In presence of manufactured goods from West Pakistan, the domestic industries of Bangla Desh failed to get necessary protection. During the period 1950-51 to 1969-70, the total exports of West Pakistan to Bangla Desh were of Rs 17,086 million. The exports of West Pakistan to Bangla Desh comprised cotton piece goods, drugs and medicines, rape and mustard oils, manufactured tobacco, apart from other articles.

The impact of international and inter-regional trade was adverse to Bangla Desh economy. During the fifties, the balance of international and inter-regional trade of Bangla Desh was characterized by surplus which resulted in net outflow of resources. During the period from 1950-51 to 1959-60, the net outflow of resources from Bangla Desh was of Rs 1,814.6 million. On the other hand, during the same period, West Pakistan received net inflow of resources, in form of deficit in trade, of Rs 2,465.0 million. Since for Pakistan as a whole, during the same period, net inflow of resources, in form of deficit in trade, was of Rs 650.4 million only, West Pakistan received not only this inflow but also the outflow of resources from Bangla Desh. Subsequently, during the sixties, although the balance of international and inter-regional trade of Bangla Desh was also characterized by deficit, it was relatively much smaller compared to that of West Pakistan. During 1960-61 to 1969-70, the net inflow of resources, in form of deficit in trade, was of Rs 4,610.7 million to Bangla Desh compared to that of Rs 13,141.2 million to West Pakistan. The net inflow of resources, during this period, to Bangla Desh was hardly one-third of that to West Pakistan.

Central Government pursued a policy of regional discrimination in foreign aid which was required to accelerate the development of the economy. Pakistan received foreign aid for the development of both the regions, since foreign governments and international institutions took into consideration the requirements of the economy of Bangla Desh also.   However, since the whole aid was not specified for projects, the Central Government was able to allocate according to her own decisions, which failed to consider adequately the requirements of Bangla Desh.   During the fifties, 1950-51 to 1959-60, the Central Government allocated foreign aid of Rs 930 million only to Bangla Desh compared to Rs 4,080 million to West Pakistan.   The foreign aid received by Bangla Desh was hardly one-third of the foreign aid received by West Pakistan.   Subsequently, also, the situation did not improve.   Instead, the relative allocation of foreign aid to Bangla Desh must have deteriorated.   The balance of international and inter-regional trade of Bangla Desh which roughly indicated the trend in foreign assistance, it may be recalled, was hardly one-third of that of West Pakistan.   Further, the allocation of foreign exchange, in the form of loans and grants, at the government level was also marked by regional discrimination.   During the entire period of two decades, 1950-51 to 1969-70, while Bangla Desh received foreign exchange of Rs 1,651.9 million only, West Pakistan received Rs 2,758.5 million.   Bangla Desh received foreign exchange loans and grants 40 per cent less than that received by West Pakistan.   International institutions and the foreign governments must not have expected such distribution. Apparently, the Central Government transferred substantial portions of foreign aid meant for Bangla Desh to West Pakistan.

Since Bangla Desh has now emerged as an independent country, the exploitation of her economy, which forced economic backwardness, comes to an end.   In view of this, the future strategy for the development of Bangla Desh economy can be determined.   Firstly, Bangla Desh can now adequately develop her physical infrastructure facilities which shall provide necessary external economics to both public and private sector projects, and shall particularly stimulate private investments. Secondly, Bangla Desh can now utilize the whole of export earning for her own economy.   Further, a more suitable direction of trade can be pursued so as to increase foreign exchange earnings.   The loss from not having trade with some countries can be replaced by gains through trade with them.   Thirdly, the structure of imports can be suitably modified so as to meet the necessary foreign resource requirements of domestic economy.   Fourthly, trade with West Pakistan can be replaced by trade with other countries, which may bring her foreign exchange.   Also, the structure of trade which presented expansion of domestic industries can be drastically changed so that domestic industries may get necessary protection.   Finally, Bangla Desh shall be able to directly negotiate for foreign aid and utilize the whole of it for development of her own economy. The prospects of the development of Bangla Desh economy are now bright.

NOTE : The figures provided in the paper are based on data available in: Five-year Plan Documents of Pakistan; Pakistan Economic Surveys; Monthly Statistical Bulletins, Pakistan; and Pakistan Statistical Year-books.

P. C. JOSHI

LAND REFORM: AN URGENT PROBLEM IN BANGLA DESH

AMONG THE MAJOR problems facing Bangla Desh after its liberation, the land problem is the most basic and also the most massive. Indeed, it constitutes the hard core of the larger problem of transforming a poor, agrarian country into a prosperous, modern nation.

I

The land problem has many dimensions: an excessively high man-land ratio further aggravated by increasing population pressure and by general backwardness including specially the lack of industrial development; an inequitous and retrograde land system which contributes to low agricultural productivity and which is made more rigid and inequitous by technological backwardness on the one hand and lack of occupational diversification on the other; a rigid social structure inherited from the colonial and *zamindari* period which still supports parasitic and unproductive ways of life based on unearned incomes from landed property, usury and trade, and which thwarts the growth of genuine entrepreneurship; the continuing weakness of techno-economic infra-structure, education and general enlightenment which strengthens over-dependence on land,

and the low level of aspirations and which also perpetuates the overall weakness of the human factor as a productive force.

Considering the fact that the total social situation is inimical to growth and development, it is safe to conclude that the land problem has to be attacked on several fronts. The emergence of an independent Bangla Desh provides a rare opportunity to initiate a set of new policies, both short-term and long-term, which may help break the vicious circle of poverty and stimulate growth and development. Agrarian reform measures need to be assigned a high priority in any minimum programme of development and nation-building.

It may be recalled that during more than two decades of the existence of undivided Pakistan, the West Pakistan-dominated administration postponed most of the urgently needed agrarian reforms both in the East and the West. The deep conservatism in land policy shown by the landlord-dominated ruling elite stood in marked contrast to the tradition of agrarian radicalism which was an important element in East Bengal politics since the days of the struggle against British rule. *The East Bengal State Acquisition and Tenancy Act of 1950* was the product of this radical trend. But the cause of land reform suffered because of lukewarm implementation of this Act, and the takeover by the West Pakistan military junta even resulted in a retreat from the accepted provisions of this Act. (The most glaring in this respect was the upward revision of the ceiling on land holdings from 33 acres to 125 acres for East Bengal after the military takeover.) The agrarian situation deteriorated as a result of pro-landlord bias of the ruling class which was not merely indifferent but hostile to urgent implementation of agrarian reforms. Severity of the agrarian problem was also due to the discriminatory policy pursued by the military junta with a view to exploiting East Bengal as an agrarian hinterland of West Pakistan. As between West and East Pakistan, much greater attention was given to the building up of a techno-economic structure of development in the former than in the latter.

It is not difficult to gauge the consequences of this type of domination and discrimination, both at the economic and political levels, on the agrarian society of East Bengal. As a result of arrested development and the continuing overpressure on land, the story so familiar under the British rule was repeated —a story of accentuated competition for land, of persistence of non-cultivating and unproductive landlordism, of deteriorating landlord-tenant relations and of increasing distress of small peasants and labourers on account of indebtedness, and uncertainty as well as insecurity of employment.

If the widespread agrarian tension in Bangla Desh did not assume the form of a major peasant upheaval, it was partly because of the reign of terror which was let loose by the military junta over East Bengal. It was also because the need for multiclass mobilization on the more immediate issue of political liberation from West Pakistan domination overshadowed all other issues for the time being. It would be wrong, however, to ignore the powerful urge for basic reforms in the economic structure which was one of the basic motive forces of the national liberation struggle and which was also responsible for its wide sweep, tenancity and endurance.

The transformation of what had been treated as a colony of West Pakistan into an independent and sovereign Bangla Desh marks the fulfilment of the immediate political objective. Now that an independent statehood has been achieved, the basic economic and social urges underlying the political struggle are bound to come more and more to the surface. The challenge facing the national leadership of Bangla Desh is to articulate these urges and to channelize them in a constructive direction. Agrarian reform against this background emerges as the first essential step for initiating a new course of economic, social, and political development. It also appears as an essential requirement for political unification of the national-democratic and socialist forces in Bangla Desh. Indeed, the criterion for distinguishing between conservative nationalism on the one hand and radical nationalism on the other is provided by the programme of land reforms implemented in the best interests of the rural masses.

For a predominantly agrarian Bangla Desh, much more than for any other underdeveloped country, the many-sided importance of land reform cannot be over-emphasized. It should be remembered that the old order in Bangla Desh was based on landlord dominance which contributed not only to economic stagnation but also to social conservatism and to political reaction. Land reform, therefore, appears as the essential basis not only for a new economy but also for a new society and a new polity. Whether or not the fruits of economic growth in future are monopolized by a small minority or are diffused among the rural masses; whether or not there is a decisive turn from the parasitism and inertia of the Zamindari period towards a dynamic and egalitarian ethos; whether or not there emerges a firm social and economic base for a non-militaristic and democratic polity; indeed the very nature and direction of modern development in Bangla Desh is likely to be conditioned by the choices that it now makes in regard to its agrarian institutional pattern.

II

The agrarian problem concerns primarily the rural masses comprising three major classes of agrarian society, viz. (1) the tenants and sharecroppers, (2) the small owner-cultivators, and (3) the landless labourers. The nature of the agrarian problem, that is to say the nature of the agrarian class structure, may be characterized by regional variations and peculiarities. Further, there may exist considerable overlapping of all the three categories. But, fundamentally speaking, the agrarian problem in Bangla Desh as a whole assumes three major forms: (1) the problem of unproductive and non-cultivating landlordism; (2) the problem of small and dwarf holdings; and (3) the problem of insecurity of employment for landless labourers.

The Problem of Landlordism

It may be recalled that the *East Bengal State Acquisition and Tenancy Act of 1950* sought to put an end only to the rent-receiving interests of original *zamindars* and to re-establish contact between the cultivating tenant and the government. The curtailment of *zamindari* rights, however, was not the same thing as the curtailment of landlordism for two main reasons. The original *zamindar* was permitted to hold an area of more than 33 acres (which was later increased to 125 acres) as his personal (*khas*) holding. The management of these *khas* lands was generally left by *zamindars* to their paid agents (*gumashtas*) who in turn got them cultivated on lease basis by the *bargadars*. Where the original *zamindar* was a Hindu who migrated to India, the land was either transferred to or captured by the under-proprietors or the paid agents of *zamindars.* The transfer of ownership/management, however, left the mode of cultivation largely unaltered.

The other loophole of the Act which gave a lease of life to landlordism was the definition of the cultivating tenant as a tenure-holder who cultivated with the help of *bargadars.* In other words, in respect of large proportion of *khas* holdings as well as *tenant* holdings the legal owners or those having owner-like possession continued to thrive as non-cultivating, rent-receiving landlords without active interest in the productive management of land or in the organization of agriculture. The Act of 1950, therefore, only removed the top layer of big *zamindars* but it did not make a serious dent into the problem of sub-infeudation which was the bane of the land system in Bengal since the British period. Thus tenancy signifying discrepancy between ownership and operation of land which earlier existed on a wide scale continues to exist today, even though the precise magnitude of it is not known.

According to the Pakistan Agricultural Census of 1960, area rented from others as a proportion of total cultivated area amounts to about 18 per cent. (It should be noted that most of this area is rented on the basis of share-cropping tenancy; area rented on share-cropping basis as proportion of total cultivated area amounts to 16.2 per cent.) This figure, however, relates only to open tenancy; and, as many village surveys and studies by economists have revealed *disguised* or *underground tenancy* has emerged as an important feature of the agrarian situation of East Bengal specially after the Estate Acquisition and Tenancy Act of 1950 was introduced. Thus, apart from open tenancy amounting to 18 per cent, it is quite plausible that "disguised" tenancy may account for a much larger proportion of cultivated area. This should be considered as a safe inference in the light of Indian experience in the recent past. The scope for tenancy going underground was provided by the fact that the definition of the cultivated tenant adopted in the Act of 1950 "turned the *bargadar* into an agricultural labourer so far as the law was concerned" (Andrus and Mohammad, *Economy of Pakistan*, 1958). In other words, open and concealed tenancy together may range anywhere between 30 to 40 per cent of the total cultivated area.

It is not only the substantial magnitude of tenancy which constitutes a serious socio-economic problem. The gravity of the problem assumes a new significance if one remembers that the major proportion of the tenanted area comprises subsistence lease by small producers rather than commercial lease by large producers. (According to the Pakistan Census of Agriculture, 1960, of the total area rented from others 71.6 per cent was leased-in by cultivators having operational holdings of less than 7.5 acres, 26.3 per cent by cultivators in the 7.5 to under 25 acres size-group and 2.1 per cent by cultivators in the 25 acres and above size-group.) This implies that even though not all the rural poor belong to the category of tenants, there is no doubt that most of the tenants belong to the category of the rural poor. The problem of tenancy existing on a large scale poses a serious obstacle for implementing a programme which subserves the objectives of growth as well as equity.

From the past experience of Bangla Desh and of India it is also evident beyond doubt that the problem of landlordism cannot be separated from that of concentration of landownership. Unless tenancy reforms for rent reduction, security of tenure, and ownership rights for actual tillers are combined with a simultaneous enforcement of low ceilings on land holdings, the scope of tenancy persisting in disguised, if not in open, forms remains. This is because under conditions of high man-land ratio and lack of alternative avenues outside agriculture, there is cut-throat competition for land among the rural masses. And in a situation where the returns from backward agriculture are low and the farming operations are hard and arduous, large ownership holdings are invariably associated with high incidence of tenancy, with tenants eking out their subsistence under inequitous terms and conditions. So long as basic economic forces (labour surplus and scarcity of land and capital) tend to work against the interests of rural masses who have low bargaining power, economic measures like tenancy and land ceilings have necessarily to operate in conjunction with non-economic forces like support of political groups and tenant organizations in order to tilt the economic balance in favour of the tenants. In other words, without a power balance at all levels in favour of the rural poor, there is no prospect of any reforms from above serving the interests of the actual tillers of land who carry the burden of high rents and other types of exactions.

The Problem of Small Farmers

The problem of landlordism is also closely connected with the predominance of small farms in the agricultural economy of Bangla Desh. It is important to note, that unlike many regions of India, Bangla Desh is a country of small farmers *as well as* small farms. According to the Pakistan Agricultural Census of 1960, of the total cultivated area in Bangla Desh about 62 per cent existed in the form of operated holdings of below 7.5 acres; and of the total operational holdings in Bangla

Desh, about 90 per cent were in size-groups of below 7.5 acres. It may further be noted that about 50 per cent of the total operational holdings, which accounted for only 16 per cent of the total cultivated area, were in the size-groups of below 2.5 acres.

It is important to note that in the context of serious economic and natural uncertainties of small peasant cultivation in Bangla Desh, every small, specially dwarf, producer is a potential share-cropper or an agricultural labourer. The precarious nature of small peasant cultivation involves continuous need for credit, a situation which provides a fertile soil for the emergence of *usurious landlordism*. Andrus and Mohammad in their book *The Economy of Pakistan* (1958) suggest that in Bangla Desh after the eclipse of the Hindu moneylender, the agriculturist in need of credit has either to sell portions of his holding or take recourse to mortgage of a portion of his holding in complete usufructuary mortgage. "In most cases, the debtor is retained as a *bargadar* on the mortgaged land on a share-cropper basis and thus the mortgager makes an annual profit of 50 per cent whereas the debtor obtains satisfaction of his loan at an annual rate of one-fifteenth or one-twentieth only. Even so less than one-tenth of the transfer of land in the province is reported to be under such mortgages, the rest being sold outright. This is despite the fact that almost 100,000 transfers under usufructuary mortgages may be recorded each year. The credit situation in the province would thus appear to be very serious. Indeed, the need for credit either exposes the cultivators to exploitation or reduces them to the status of landless labourers" (p. 149).

The small owner-cultivator is thus threatened with loss of his land both by natural disasters like floods and droughts, etc., and economic instabilities like fall in the prices of agricultural commodities. He is unable to build up reserves even during periods of higher prices the benefit of which goes largely "to the trader and middleman and some section of the big *zamindars* leaving the small proprietors, tenants and day-labourers in almost the same situation as before" (Andrus and Mohammad, *op. cit.*, p. 153).

Thus, even if rights of ownership or owner-like possession are conferred on small tenant cultivators, the threat of re-emergence of landlord-tenant relations is bound to continue. In order to remove this threat it will be necessary that small producer economy is supported by a wider institutional framework of cooperation which neutralizes its resources constraints and organizational weaknesses and at the same time draws it into the process of sustained growth and development. Small peasant economy thus would require not merely a *protective* framework which at best helps its survival at a low level of productivity. It would also require a *developmental* framework which allows for technical progress and, consequently, for rising levels of productivity of both land and labour. Such a framework, though allowing for individual peasant ownership and/or of cultivation of land, will have to make use of cooperative ownership and management of capital, credit, inputs, and other social overheads. More importantly, it will have to ensure mobilization of vast, unutilized manpower for community asset-building on a basis transcending the family, and the village and involving sometimes groups of villages. A cooperative economy seems to be a necessary framework for transition from a depressed small peasant economy to a dynamic and diversified rural economy.

The Problem of Landless Labourers

Landless labourers constitute a large proportion of the total rural population in Bangla Desh. According to one estimate they constituted 15 per cent of the rural labour force of 10.7 million (Andrus and Mohammad, *op. cit.*, 1958, p. 430).[1]

It should be noted that the general backwardness of the agricultural economy precluded the existence of a well-defined class of permanent agricultural labourers which is characteristic of large producer-based agriculture. A noteworthy feature of landless labourers in the recent past was their mixed and floating status; they oscillated between pure labourer status and cultivator status. They often belong to a mixed category of tenants-cum-labourers. In other words, quite often the dividing line between labourers and tenants was very thin. They were passed off as labourers or as tenants depending upon the convenience or interest of the masters of land in the villages. The problem facing the landless class was of hard conditions of employment as much as of the uncertainty and insecurity of employment for more than half the year.

While the problem of the landless class was quite serious even in the past, recent changes like reforms of land tenure have ironically added to the insecurity of their employment. Andrus and Mohammad point out that "the ranks of agricultural labourers are being swollen with the addition of the *bargadars* who no longer hold the status of tenants, since subletting has been abolished" (Andrus and Mohammad, *op. cit.*, p. 130).

---

[1] A most recent assessment places the landless at 30 per cent of the rural population (Sivadas Banerjee, "Problems Facing Bangla Desh", *The Times of India*, 5 February 1972)

The problem of employment for the landless class as well as for the small producers may assume a more naked and grave form if in future technological transformation of agriculture takes place without a prior change in the agrarian sturcture in favour of the rural poor. It is quite certain that technological transformation may favour conversion of a part of the landless as well as of small peasants into permanent agricultural labourers. But it would also increase the proportion of the landless class without simultaneously increasing the scope for employment within the rural sector or outside.

III

To sum up, so far as the majority of the rural population consisting of small owner-cultivators, tenants and labourers are concerned, they are now facing a total disturbance in their traditional livelihood patterns. If social forces do not intervene soon enough to bring about changes in the interests of the rural masses, market forces which are already in motion may gain the upper hand and impose a pattern of development in the interest of the propertied classes.

It may further be noted that in Bangla Desh a technological break-through comparable to that of West Pakistan has not yet occurred either in terms of control of floods or the discovery of appropriate seed varieties. Since the role of technology in pushing up the traditionally low returns from agriculture has so far been insignificant, it is not surprising that technological factors have so far not played a major role in influencing the pattern of agrarian change. This situation has been undergoing change as a result of greater attention being paid to problems of technical change and progress. With a breakthrough in rice technology there is bound to come about a shift towards commercialism among the landlords and peasants operating relatively bigger holdings in Bangla Desh. These techno-economic changes may no doubt reduce to some extent the hiatus between ownership and management of land. But, the important point to emphasize is that, without any serious dent into the problem of over-pressure on land, resumption of land for direct cultivation on a large scale by large holders may have serious consequences. An inevitable decline in subsistence tenancy or smal-sized agriculture then may lead to an immediate contraction of employment opportunities, creating thus an explosive situation in rural areas. This will bring in its wake not only economic problems; it will also aggravate political tension and discontent in the countryside.

Against this background land reform in the coming period appears not only to be an economic but also a political necessity. The war of liberation from rule of the military junta was fought with the active mobilization of the small peasants and the landless class. Neither economic recovery nor the war against poverty can now be won without the active involvement of these very classes. They constitute the overwhelming majority of the new nation; and it is idle to imagine that they can be mobilized for growth and development in the given economic framework of a landlord-dominated small peasant economy. Nor can they be drawn into the process of growth and development through any future transition into a rich peasant or large producer-dominated economy.

In the coming period, there will be a general demand for land reform with a view to putting an end to landlordism. But the process of anti-feudal reforms can either lead to the emergence of a rich peasant economy or of an economic framework serving the interests of the rural masses. Whether land reforms are implemented in the interests of the rural poor or of the emerging capitalistic classes will however depend on the overall balance of political forces. The general political situation after political liberation can be said to provide a context favourable to radical rather than conservative type of land reforms.

NOTES :—

1. For a more detailed analysis of the agrarian structure before the formation of Bangla Desh, see the author's paper "Land Reform and Agrarian Change in India and Pakistan Since 1947" in Ratna Dutta and P.C. Joshi (Eds), *Studies in Asian Social Development*, Number I, Tata Mc Graw-Hill, 1971.

2. For select bibliography see Appendix, at the end of the book.

B.N. GANGULI

SOME ECONOMIC PROBLEMS OF BANGLA DESH

ONE SHOULD HAVE no difficulty in imagining that the Bangla Desh economy has to confront difficult problems of a transition from war to peace. There is first the problem of setting the wheels of the agricultural economy moving. The standing *aman* rice crop, where it has not been destroyed, has to be harvested, available supplies controlled, if not rationed, and special measures taken to even out supplies as between the surplus and the deficit areas. Relief supplies of food augmenting the total availability may appropriately be used, as far as possible, to feed the concentrations of population in the cities and elsewhere. Supplies of edible oil, kerosene, and salt have to flow to meet urgent requirements. Quick-growing winter crops of vegetables and fish should be easily available as valuable supplements to a meagre rice diet. Bangla Desh is known for its poultry and eggs. Fortunately, a new agricultural season awaits the harvesting of winter rice, and considering the character of the last monsoon, one may, on the whole, take an optimistic view of the yield of *rabi* crop which, one should presume, will be selected wisely on the basis of an emergency crop planning. One can safely count upon the amazing resourcefulness and industry of the

Bangla Desh peasant who can rise to the occasion against the heaviest of odds, provided he cbtains credit, seeds, fertilizers, and agricultural implements where these may be lacking.

Agriculture, fisheries, poultry farming, on the one hand, and animal husbandry, plantation agriculture, and horticulture to a limited extent, on the other hand, deserve immediate attention. They constitute the lynch-pin of the Bangla Desh economy and determine the economic fortunes of the masses who have now come into their own in Bangla Desh.

The pattern of what should happen has already emerged in the form of the demand, for instance, for the activization of barter trade between Sylhet and Assam to ease the economic difficulties of the people of Sylhet. Sylhet tea could be offered a good market at the Gauhati tea auction. If reports have to be believed, even prior to the 14-day war, tobacco, jute, vegetables, and pulses were moving across the border on the north-west to be exchanged for essential consumer goods. There is no reason why fish, eggs, and vegetables in small quanities as well as bamboo and *gur* (from date palm) cannot find a ready market across the border.

The essential safeguards, however, are the following: (1) to prevent distress sales and exploitation by unscrupulous dealers; (2) to ensure fair terms of barter; and (3) to have regulated marketing in such a way that Bangla Desh people get the scarce consumer goods like salt, matches, and edible oil in limited quantities.

The best way of serving the rural masses and making them restart agricultural operations would be, among other things, to ensure the supply of credit or relief in kind: food (where necessary); seeds, fertilizer, agricultural implements (where needed); locally available building materials. Floating manpower should be organized into a kind of land-army under the leadership of the student wing of the Mukti Bahini to undertake the task of agricultural rehabilitation. A large and disciplined task force is required to repair and rebuild rural dwellings, to repair stretches of local roads and small bridges, to clear the navigation channels essential for the local agricultural economy and, above all, on a priority basis, to assist the harvesting of the *aman* rice crop. Such a land army can also help in barter trade; supply of the working capital in agriculture in the form of seeds, fertilizer, and implements; supply of the farmers' barest needs of consumer goods, etc. A plan for such a task force can be worked out in conjunction with the plan of rehabilitation of displaced persons.

Basically, the Bangla Desh economy is a rice-jute economy. There is urgent need for the assembling and transportation of such raw jute as may be lying scattered because of the dislocation of movement of supplies and possible disposal. Stocks lying at Chittagong and Chalna have to be lifted. Stocks dispersed in inland centres have to be *located* and assembled. Shipping and reinsurance facilities have to be provided. Export of raw jute, if necessary through the Calcutta port, on behalf of the Bangla Desh Government, should immediately be organized in order to enable it to earn much-needed foreign exchange. The Bangla Desh Government may organize a jute marketing board for this purpose. Bangla Desh's golden fibre has a specialized market in Dundee. *Reuter* reported recently that thousands of jute workers employed in Dundee for the manufacture of yarn for mainly carpet-making now face a serious restriction in working hours because of shortage of raw jute from Bangla Desh. A delegation from Dundee will visit Calcutta and Dacca to discuss this problem. It is an urgent task for both Bangla Desh Government and Dundee to deal with this urgent problem with the assistance and sympathy of the Government of India.

While one thinks of the rehabilitation of Bangla Desh's agriculture, one cannot dismiss from one's mind the fact that agriculture in this new nation has been the victim of comparative neglect and exploitation through the maintenance of relatively low farm prices as compared with the prices of industrial products, particularly the prices of processed or semi-processed agricultural products earning foreign exchange. This process of exploitation will naturally come to an end in a people's republic. At the same time, one should take an optimistic view of the technological possibilities of Bangla Desh's agriculture so far as rice yields are concerned. The Green Revolution has not occurred in Bangla Desh.

In Pakistan the wheat yield registered in the last few years an increase of 63 per cent as compared with the output in 1960-1965. During the same period the new variety of IRRI Pakistan rice registered a yield of 14.1 maunds per acre, compared with the yield of only 10.1 maunds in 1960-65. In Bangla Desh—*par excellence* the land of rice—the average yield per acre was 12.1 maunds in 1960-65, while the highest yield recorded so far in recent years has been only 12.6 maunds. The rice variety that suited Pakistan did not succeed in Bangla Desh for a number of reasons. One reason mentioned in a recent ECAFE report was that the poor Bengali farmer with his small holding did not have the purchasing power to buy fertilizer. Another reason was that he did not enjoy the necessary irrigation facilities. One should be reasonably certain that such reasons will no longer be permitted to be valid in Bangla Desh.

But what is perhaps more a matter of determined long-range planning is the evolution of a monsoon variety of rice adapted to local conditions, particularly the flooding of land during the monsoon season. Agronomists and plant geneticists in Bangla Desh and India should pool their scientific skills and resources to deal with this problem. Once the Green Revolution gets under way in Bangla Desh, near self-sufficiency in food can hardly be a problem for this new nation. But if one industry allied to agriculture that has to develop rapidly in the near future it should be fertilizer production[1]. Attention has also to be paid to lift irrigation in certain areas and control of floods in others on the basis of small labour-intensive projects, in the first instance, before the overall bigger problems of flood control can be handled on a regional or sub-regional basis. (Flood control, irrigation, and power generation can very well be planned and coordinated on a mutually advantageous bilateral basis between India and Bangla Desh.)

One aspect of the opening up of internal communications deserves special attention against the background of agriculture, rural trade, and distribution as well as rural employment in the very short period. Many have been thinking of the restoration of river transportation that once linked Assam with West Bengal through the arterial river routes of the lower Ganges Delta now Bangla Desh. It is clear that the restoration of the economic pattern prior to partition, according to which what is now Bangla Desh was an intermediary hinterland, is out of the question. Nevertheless, the internal waterways of Bangla Desh linking Assam, West Bengal, and Bangla Desh can serve the same function as the

---

[1] There is one fertilizer unit in Bangla Desh at present.

Rhine and the Danube, and navigation and transit trade can be easily regulated on a mutually advantageous basis through a joint maritime commission according to international conventions and practices. Such a Commission can also deal with a possible co-ordination of the coastal trade of Bangla Desh with that of India.

The opening up of a vast transit trade, linking with the foreign trade of Bangla Desh, can be an important source of revenue by way of tolls at various points and service charges in accordance with international norms and practices. What is of immediate significance for Bangla Desh is, however, the restoration of navigation on the smaller rivers and waterways by countryboats and crude barges, before one can think of fuel-driven river craft. This will open up channels of internal trade and distribution so vital for agricultural activity in the immediate future. It will also provide employment on a fairly large scale as time passes, without much investment of capital. This would also seem to be a matter of top priority, pending the repair of roads, repair or replacement of vital bridges and culverts and the restoration of the railway links, all of which would take time and absorb scarce investible resources. One is sure that the Bangla Desh Government will do the needful and perhaps make a beginning with the assembling of riverine transport workers and seeking their advice and cooperation in order to undertake this fairly gigantic task. It is heartening to learn that the Indian Navy has already undertaken the exacting work of clearing of blocked entrances to Bangla Desh ports and the numerous waterways by removing sunken ships and gunboats as well as mines. It is understood that the possible sites where mines may have been located have already been surveyed.

One should imagine that there is the difficult problem of fuel supply to set the wheels of the Bangla Desh economy moving. The economy immediately needs coal and diesel oil in quantities that are the minimum necessary for industry and power generation. There is the difficult problem of fuel for domestic consumption. Firewood and other kinds of fuel may have to be thought of till other possibilities emerge. Natural gas supplies have to be restored and augmented. The highest priority will naturally be given to the importation of fuel required to operate the power stations which must reach peak load as early as possible. Bangla Desh's petroleum requirements estimated at 150,000 tonnes a month will have to be met by the Indian Oil Corporation till the damaged 1.5 million-tonne refinery at Chittagong is put back into Commission.

The future pattern of industrial development in Bangla Desh will crystallize as time passes and the perspective becomes clear. There are 33 jute mills in Bangla Desh which have to be restarted, but they have now to be adapted mostly to the requirements of export trade, whereas a change in the direction of trade is probable on the estimation of current trends. Cotton textile mills will face the problem of raw cotton. The possibilities of increasing cultivation of long-staple cotton in Bangla Desh have to be explored. Cardboard and newsprint production can profitably expand. All these developments, however, will take time and depend upon favourable conditions of capital formation on the initiative of the Bangla Desh Government, the *modus operandi* of which will depend upon State policy.

There is no ground for pessimism about the prospects of

capital formation so vitally necessary for both agricultural and industrial development. Bangla Desh has been exporting every year Rs 90 crores worth of goods to Pakistan including tea (Rs 23 crores). They will fetch higher prices when they are exported to foreign countries. Part of the exports will, however, be domestically consumed, because the masses will expect a rise in the abnormally low levels of living. We may add to this Rs 140 crores worth of jute exports, which may be a lower figure in view of the recent currency re-alignments. On the other hand, Bangla Desh has been importing Rs 138 crores worth of goods mostly from Pakistan at inflated prices. The import bill now is likely to be much less.

One may, therefore, look for a sizable export surplus which was otherwise drained away as rent, interest, and profits to Pakistan and which would now be available for (1) State capital formation to raise the level of productivity, employment and income, and/or (2) higher social consumption. Obviously, however, the gigantic task of repair of damage, reconstruction, redevelopment, resettlement, and economic recovery can be financed only with substantial foreign aid.

B.B. BHATTACHARYA

TRADE STRUCTURE OF BANGLA DESH

ONE OF THE major factors that helped in widening of the regional disparity between erstwhile East Pakistan, now Bangla Desh, and West Pakistan was the commercial policy of the then federal government of Pakistan. The twin objectives of the federal commercial policy were to utilize the surplus foreign exchange earnings of Bangla Desh for the development of West Pakistan on the one hand and to use Bangla Desh as a colonial market for industrial products of West Pakistan on the other. These objectives were fulfilled basically through the artificial restriction of foreign imports of Bangla Desh which created a foreign exchange surplus and also promoted the West Pakistani products into Bangla Desh market. The structure of trade of Bangla Desh, foreign as well as the inter-wing, that resulted from this policy was beneficial to West Pakistan at the cost of the economy of Bangla Desh.

The imposition of trade embargo with India after the 1965 war between the two countries led to a further deterioration of the economy of Bangla Desh. India was the largest customer of Bangla Desh's two major export commodities, viz. raw jute and fish. In the case of fish the lack of Indian demand reduced the total exports of fish by more than 50 per cent

and consequently the output also went down. The increase
in domestic production of manufactured jute goods and the
diversification of export market did compensate to some
extent the loss due to non-exporting of raw jute to India.
However, the potential loss was very high if due consideration
was given to the excess demand for raw jute in India in the
late sixties and the excess capacity of raw jute production
in Bangla Desh over and above the domestic requirement
and non-Indian foreign demand.

In terms of imports the loss due to non-trading with India
was even more severe. Bangla Desh used to import from
India some essential commodities like coal, limestone, cement,
minerals, metals, chemicals, engineering goods, etc., which
were essential for industrialization. With the imposition of
trade embargo with India, these commodities began to be
imported from far away places with a much higher transportation cost. As for example, coal which used to be imported
from the Eastern India coal belt was imported all the way
from Poland and China after the embargo. Similarly, Meghalaya
limestone which used to be imported to Bangla Desh cement
factory by a one-hour river boat journey was replaced by
limestone from Baluchistan, 1,500 miles away. Consequently,
Bangla Desh had to pay much more for the same quantity
of imports. West Pakistan, however, did not suffer much due
to the trade embargo since the shares of India in the exports
and imports of West Pakistan were negligible in 1964-65.
In fact, the embargo helped West Pakistan because it enabled
it to replace most of the Indian commodities in Bangla Desh
market by West Pakistani products.

With Independence, Bangla Desh would persue a commercial
policy suited for its own economic development and hence the

structure of its foreign trade is likely to change substantially. Broadly, three factors have special significance in this context. First is the political separation of Bangla Desh from West Pakistan. Prior to Independence, the imports of Bangla Desh from West Pakistan used to be roughly of the same magnitude as from the rest of the world, and the exports to West Pakistan used to be much smaller than that from abroad. If trade is to take place between them now, it would involve foreign exchange, in which case both the volume and the composition of trade between them may change drastically. Bangla Desh now may dispense with most of the non-essential consumer goods imports from West Pakistan, and also may replace many other import commodities from alternative sources with cheaper cost. West Pakistan, likewise, may cut down its imports of tea and manufactured jute goods from Bangla Desh which together constitute more than 50 per cent of its imports from Bangla Desh.

A second important factor in the future trade pattern of Bangla Desh would be the reopening of trade with India. Under present conditions, India is likely to emerge as the largest trading partner of Bangla Desh, at least in the immediate future. This may be partly due to the reopening of original trade pattern that existed before the embargo, which had accounted for roughly 15 per cent of exports and 7 per cent of imports of Bangla Desh in 1964-65. It may also be partly due to the replacement of West Pakistani products in Bangla Desh by Indian products, particularly those of engineering goods, light machinery, chemicals, drugs, cements, limestone, and cotton textiles, etc., in which India enjoys comparative cost advantages in Bangla Desh.

Finally, the process of industrialization of Bangla Desh

would itself be a major factor in altering its trade structure. Presently, the imports of Bangla Desh are heavily tilted towards consumer goods, particularly those from West Pakistan. The process of industrialization, under a foreign exchange constraint, would shift the emphasis to the imports of capital goods, industrial raw materials, and other essential commodities like fuel, coal, fertilizers, etc., which are essential for economic development. The major problem of Bangla Desh would be to balance the increasing demand for imports, particularly of capital goods, by its foreign exchange earnings which accrue at present almost entirely by the exports of traditional items. The aim of this essay is to analyze briefly the basic trade structure of Bangla Desh that it would inherit from erstwhile East Pakistan and to discuss the likely changes in it by the three factors mentioned above.

II

In this section we shall discuss the overall trends in exports and imports of Bangla Desh or erstwhile East Pakistan. The commodity patterns of exports and imports would be discussed in subsequent sections.

The foreign trade of Bangla Desh, before the trade embargo with India, was always favourable except for the years, 1963-64 and 1964-65. During the period 1949-50 to 1965-66, Bangla Desh earned on an average Rs 250 million worth foreign exchange a year from trade. The average annual rates of growth of exports and imports during this period were roughly 8 per cent and 10 per cent respectively. The imposition of trade embargo with India affected both exports and imports of Bangla Desh much more severely than those of West Pakistan. Exports of Bangla Desh almost stagnated at an

average annual growth rate of 2 per cent from 1965-66 to
1969-70. Imports after initial setback picked up again in
1968-69. The average annual growth rate during the period
1965-66 to 1969-70 became roughly 9 per cent. Imports
started increasing at a faster rate than exports. Consequently,
the positive balance of trade started declining and by 1968-69
the foreign trade of Bangla Desh turned unfavourable.

Bangla Desh's exports to India in 1964-65 were around
Rs 200 million or roughly 15 per cent of total foreign exports.
The bulk of exports to India used to constitute only two
items: raw jute and fish. West Pakistan had no demand for

TABLE I

EXPORTS AND IMPORTS OF BANGLA DESH

(Rs. million)

Year	Foreign Trade			Trade with West Pakistan		
	Exports	Imports	Balance of Trade	Exports	Imports	Balance of Trade
1949-50	629	385	+ 244	20	140	—120
1954-55	732	320	+ 412	198	305	—107
1957-58	988	736	+ 252	270	702	—432
1960-61	1259	1014	+ 245	364	817	—453
1962-63	1249	1019	+ 230	425	865	—440
1964-65	1268	1702	— 430	537	875	—338
1965-66	1514	1328	+ 186	652	1209	—557
1966-67	1575	1566	+ 9	737	1344	—605
1967-68	1484	1327	+ 157	785	1233	—448
1968-69	1543	1850	— 307	867	1343	—466
1969-70	1670	1813	— 143	916	1652	—736

Sources: *Statistical Digest of East Pakistan* 1966, East Pakistan Bureau
of Statistics; *Pakistan Economic Survey* 1970-71, Ministry of Finance,
Government of Pakistan.

these commodities, and the loss of exports to India could only
be compensated by the increase in exports to other countries. However, the increase in the exports to major alternative
markets—Ceylon in the case of fish and the USA and Europe
in the case of raw jute—were not sufficient to compensate
for the loss of exports to India. Thus the index number
of quantum of exports (1954-55 = 100) declined from 125 in
1964-65 to 118 in 1965-66 and 114 in 1966-67.

Imports from India in 1964-66 were around Rs 125 million
or roughly 7 per cent of total foreign imports. The bulk of
imports from India used to constitute some essential items
like minerals and machinery. As there was very little import
substitution in these items, the imports from India were replaced by imports from West Pakistan and other sources.
India enjoyed comparative cost advantage and therefore
replacement of Indian commodities by imports from other
sources resulted in inflating the value of imports without
increasing the quantum. Thus, while the value of imports and
the index numbers of unit value of imports (1954-55 = 100)
were both showing an upward trend after 1965, the index
numbers of quantum of imports (1954-55 = 100) had actually
declined after 1965.[1]

While foreign trade suffered due to the stoppage of trade
with India, West Pakistan's exports to Bangla Desh almost
doubled after 1964-65. West Pakistan was a close competitor
of India in many commodities in Bangla Desh market, and
hence, the trade embargo became a boon to West Pakistani
products in Bangla Desh market. Bangla Desh's exports to

1 The data on the index numbers of unit value and quantum of exports
and imports are given in *Monthly Statistical Bulletin*, March 1969, C.S.O.,
Government of Pakistan.

West Pakistan could not increase at a comparable rate and, as a result, the regional balance of trade became more unfavourable for Bangla Desh.

TABLE 2

DIRECTIONS OF FOREIGN TRADE OF BANGLA DESH

(Relative shares in per cent)

Country and Regions	1963-64		1968-69	
	Exports	Imports	Exports	Imports
USA	10	35	14	35
ECM	20	12	21	23
UK	14	14	14	9
Eastern Europe	6	2	6	6
Middle East	2	5	3	1
Australia	5	2	4	1
Japan	—	—	3	15
Other Asian countries	20	21	19	8
South America	3	—	4	—
Africa	—	—	10	—
Others	20	9	1	2
TOTAL	100	100	100	100

SOURCE: The relative shares in 1963-64 are obtained from *Statistical Digest of East Pakistan*, 1964, and those of 1968-69 are obtained from *Monthly Statistical Bulletin*, March 1969, Government of Pakistan.

Combining both foreign and inter-wing trades, the shares of exports and imports to G.N.P. at factor cost were 5.3 per cent and 4 per cent respectively in 1949-50. By 1964-65 the relative shares increased to 14 per cent and 10 per cent respectively. After the trade embargo with India the pattern changed. The ratio of exports to G.N.P. at factor cost declined to 10 per cent and that of imports increased to 14 per cent in 1969-70.[2] Thus,

2 The data on G.N.P. at factor costs for 1949-50 and 1964-65 are taken from Sengupta and that for 1969-70 are obtained from *Pakistan Economic Survey*, 1970-71.

without making structural changes for industrialization, Bangla Desh was made to depend more and more on imports.

It is evident that most of foreign trade of Bangla Desh was with hard currency nations. Further, there had not been much structural changes in the direction of foreign trade between the years 1963-64 and 1968-69.

III

The composition of exports and imports of Bangla Desh reflects a classical colonial pattern and as such needs a structural transformation. Nearly the whole of Bangla Desh's export depends on three traditional commodities: jute (both raw and manufactured), tea and fish. These three items together account for 95 per cent of foreign exports and 55 per cent of exports to West Pakistan (see Tables 3 and 4). On the import side more than 50 per cent are consumer goods. The ratio is even higher in the case of imports from West Pakistan.

TABLE 3

COMPOSITION OF BANGLA DESH'S FOREIGN EXPORTS

Item	1954-55		1967-68	
	Per cent share	Quantity	Per cent share	Quantity
Raw Jute	80	917 ('000 tons)	51	667 ('000 tons)
Jute manufactured goods	3	—	40	14 ('000 tons)
Fish	4.5	606 ('000 cwt.)	3.5	290 ('000 cwt.)
Tea	8	26 ('000 lbs)	1	1 ('000 lbs)
Cotton textiles	—	—	2	—
Leather	—	—	.5	—
Paper and paper board	—	—	.5	—

SOURCES: Same as for Table 1.

Jute, both raw and manufactured, was the main export
earner of Bangla Desh contributing more than 90 per cent
of foreign exports and 20 per cent of exports to West Pakistan
in 1967-68.   In the beginning almost all raw jute production
of Bangla Desh used to be exported and out of the exports
about 90 per cent used to be sent to India alone.   Later, with
the growing selfsufficiency of India in raw jute production
and the drive for the diversification of the raw jute exports
markets of Bangla Desh reduced the relative share of India

TABLE 4

COMPOSITIONS OF BANGLA DESH'S EXPORTS TO WEST
PAKISTAN

(Rs million)

Item	1958-59	1967-68
A. *Primary*		
Betelnuts	12	12
Spices	7	11
Wood and timbers	8	11
Others	20	63
	47	97
B. *Manufactured Goods*		
Tea	83	229
Jute goods	66	142
Paper and paper board	29	91
Matches	20	32
Leather	20	28
All other articles	24	160
	242	681
GRAND TOTAL	289	785

SOURCES: *Statistical Digest of East Pakistan*, 1964; and *Pakistan Economic Survey*, 1968-69.

and finally after the trade embargo, Bangla-Desh stopped exporting raw jute to India. The principal customers of Bangla Desh's raw jute in recent years were: the UK, the USA, France, Belgium, China, West Germany, Japan, Netherlands, Portugal, Poland, and Singapore. The combined share of these countries in the raw jute exports of Bangla Desh was more than 80 per cent in 1968-69.

Although the value of raw jute exports from Bangla Desh had been stagnant over a considerable period, the quantity of raw jute exports fluctuated around a long-run declining trend. The major factors for this declining trend were the increasing domestic production of manufactured jute goods in Bangla Desh, and the stagnancy of the world demand for raw jute (particularly the absence of demand from India).

TABLE 5

EXPORTS OF RAW JUTE AND MANUFACTURED JUTE GOODS FROM BANGLA DESH

Year	Quantity of exports of raw jute ('ooo tons)	Value of exports of raw jute (Rs million)	Exports of manufactured jute goods (abroad) (Rs million)	Exports of manufactured jute goods (West Pakistan) (Rs million)
1954-55	917	598	23	10
1957-58	854	853	91	68
1960-61	526	848	314	80
1964-65	703	845	301	105
1965-66	751	863	575	138
1966-67	598	870	588	136
1967-68	667	758	619	142
1968-69*	459	577	450	77

*Figures for 1968-69 refer to first 6 months of the period.
SOURCES: Same as for Table 4.

In 1954 Bangla Desh had only seven jute mills with an installed capacity of 3,287 looms absorbing about 400 thousand bales of raw jute. By 1968, the number of mills increased to 40 with an installed capacity of 222 thousand spindles and 19 thousand looms absorbing about 3 million bales of raw jute. The expansion of the production of manufactured jute goods led to an increase in the exports of manufactured jute goods over the years, from an insignificant amount of Rs 33 million in 1954-55 to more than Rs 750 million in 1967-68. To some extent, the decline in the potential export of raw jute was compensated by the increase in the exports of manufactured jute goods.

The production of raw jute in Bangla Desh had been stagnant over a long period, 1935 to 1969 (see Table 6). Although the jute acreage had expanded during this period, the long-run decline in yield per acre had restrained the production. The acreage of jute had been fluctuating over the years. Rice and jute were perfect competitive crops in Bangla Desh during the spring, summer and autumn farming seasons. The studies of Ahmed[3], Hussain[4], and Mallon[5] had shown that there was a close relationship between annual fluctuations in jute acreage and the jute/rice prices ratio. In the fifties the price of rice was increasing at a faster rate than that of jute. Consequently, the area under jute cultivation declined. From 1960 onwards, the trend was reversed and, consequently, the

[3] Q.K. Ahmed, "The Operation of the Export Bonus Scheme in Pakistan's Jute and Textiles", *Pakistan Development Review*, Spring 1966.

[4] S.M. Hussain, "The Effect of the Growing Constraint of Subsistence Farming on Farmers' Response to Price: A Case Study of Jute in Pakistan, *Pakistan Development Review*, Autumn 1969.

[5] R. Mallon, "Export Policy in Pakistan", *Pakistan Development Review*, Spring 1966.

TABLE 6

ACREAGE, YIELD AND PRODUCTION OF RAW JUTE AND THE
RELATIVE PRICES OF JUTE AND RICE IN BANGLA DESH
1935-1969

| Period | Raw jute | | | Index of jute/rice prices ratio average 1945-46— 1949-50 = 100) |
	Acreage ('000 acres)	Yield (maunds per acre)	Output ('000 tons)	
Average 1935-36—1939-40	2,070	15.7	1,190	135
Average 1945-46—1949-50	1,750	14.6	935	100
Average 1950-51—1954-55	1,521	17.5	980	100
Average 1955-56—1959-60	1,466	19.2	1,063	82
Average 1960-61—1964-65	1,732	16.9	1,075	116
1965-66	2,198	14.8	1,195	119
1966-67	2,165	14.4	1,143	109
1967-68	2,354	13.9	1,200	103
1968-69	2,217	12.9	1,050	98

SOURCES: R. Mallon, "Export Policy in Pakistan", *Pakistan Development Review*, Spring 1966; and *Pakistan Economic Survey*, 1968-69.

acreage of jute started expanding rapidly (see Table 6). But
in the late sixties the cut in the exports of raw jute to India
affected the price of raw jute adversely. The price of raw jute
which went up from Rs 30.25 per maund at Narayanganj
(the biggest jute market of Bangla Desh) in 1957-58 to Rs 61.82
in 1961-62 fell sharply after the trade embargo with
India to Rs 30.13 in 1966 and finally stabilized at Rs 39
in 1968.[6] The price of rice in the late sixties went up. Thus
there were clear indications of fall in jute/rice price parity in
the late sixties.

[6] Refer *Pakistan Economic Survey*, 1968-69.

Since the supply of raw jute was fairly elastic to its price, production would expand if demand would increase. A major source of new demand for raw jute would be the resumption of raw jute exports to India. There was a shortage of raw jute in India in the late sixties. A study of Mallon[7] also showed that given the yields and the costs of production of rice and jute, the farmers would prefer to cultivate jute to rice even if the demand for both commodities were increasing at the same rate. In short, given the domestic demand for raw jute, the production and exports of raw jute would increase with the increase in the export demand for raw jute.

However, the increase in the manufactured jute goods exports would be much more difficult to achieve. The costs of production of "hessian" and "sacking" jute goods in Bangla Desh were marginally lower than those in India. The comparative cost advantages of Bangla Desh in the exports of manufactured jute goods over its nearest rival India was largely due to the policy of "export bonus scheme", practised earlier.[8] The study of Mallon[9] showed that while the exports of "saking" jute goods from Bangla Desh depended more on the domestic production of "sacking", the exports of "hessian" were a function of its price. Further, the manufactured jute good were facing a stiff competition from substitute packing materials like kenef, paper, and cotton, a substantial increase in the exports of manufactured jute goods, would, therefore, be very difficult.

India and Bangla Desh also competed with each other in almost all export markets for manufactured jute goods except

[7] Mallon, op. cit.
[8] For a detailed discussion on export bonus schemes, see Ahmed, op. cit.
[9] Mallon, op. cit.

that of South Africa, which accounted for roughly 25 per cent of the exports of manufactured jutes from Bangla Desh. Therefore, in order to avoid competition, both from India and from substitute products, Bangla Desh would have to restrict the costs of production of manufactured jute goods for increasing its exports. Restraint on the cost of production of manufactured jute goods will have to be achieved by restricting the price of raw jute in the absence of increase in mill productivity. Restraining the price of raw jute may have an adverse effect on the production of raw jute due to its strong linkage with relative price of jute and rice. This has implications for exports.

Secondly, the increase in the exports of raw jute to India might also affect in the long run the exports of manufactured jute goods from Bangla Desh. The increase in the availability of raw jute in India would increase the exportable quantity of manufactured jute goods from India and could be detrimental to the long run interest of Bangla Desh. To sum up, the short-run policy of exporting raw jute to India might not entirely fulfil the long-run policy of exporting more manufactured jute goods.

The position will change entirely if India and Bangla Desh were to enter into "Indo-Bangla Desh jute community" in which case the export prices of both the countries could be protected under a common price policy. Secondly, the diversification of products and export markets would increase the world demand. There is a growing demand for manufactured jute goods in Africa and Latin America. Similarly, the demand for jute carpets and allied products in the existing export markets is also increasing quite fast. In the long run, however, Bangla Desh would have to diversify its exports by reducing its heavy dependence on the exports of raw jute goods and increase the exports of other commodities.

Fish would be one such commodity whose exports could be increased tremendously in the immediate future by exporting to India. The value of exports of fish which touched its peak in the early sixties slumped after the trade embargo. India used to import on an average about 60 per cent of fish exports of Bangla Desh. The immediate reaction to the embargo was a fall in the quantity and value of exports of fish, consequently, the output and price of fish also declined in 1966.

TABLE 7

EXPORTS OF FISH

Year	Total Exports		Exports to India	
	Quantity ('000 tons)	value (Rs million)	Quantity ('000 tons)	Value (Rs million)
1954-55	—	23.5	20.1	23.0
1957-58	11.7	14.0	11.7	14.0
1958-59	13.9	20.3	13.9	20.2
1960-61	17.1	38.2	17.1	38.0
1962-63	19.9	77.8	29.9	41.6
1964-65	14.9	46.0	14.0	27.2
1965-66	—	22.0		
1966-67	—	16.0		
1967-68	—	12.0		

SOURCES: Same as for Table 1.

Earlier tea used to be the second largest export item of Bangla Desh contributing about 8 per cent of its total exports in 1954-55. Bangla Desh's foreign exchange earnings from tea, which during the period 1951-1953 averaged more than 40 million rupees annually, had fallen to an average of Rs 6 million annually during the period 1964-1966 and subsequently the exports of tea were reduced to almost nothing. This decline in earnings resulted from stagnant production and diversion of tea from export market to domestic market and to West Pakistan. The per capita absorption of tea has gone up from .08 pounds in 1951-52 to .29 pounds in 1962-63 in Bangla Desh and in West Pakistan it increased from .45 pounds to .89 pounds during the period.[10]

TABLE 8

AREA, PRODUCTION, YIELD AND EXPORTS OF TEA

Year	Cultivated area ('000 acres)	Production (million lbs)	Yield per acre (mds)	Exports (Rs million)	
				Foreign	West Pakistan
1948-49	73.2	34.2		42.4	
1954-55	74.2	54.0		55.8	
1957-58	75.9	44.5		19.3	87.7
1960-61	78.1	42.2		1.1	110.0
1964-65	87.6	63.0	7.1	10.0	185.0
1965-66	92.0	60.3	7.7	11.0	244.0
1966-67	95.0	63.6	7.8	.8	287.0
1967-68	101.0	64.5	7.8		229.0
1968-69	103.0	62.9	7.4		

SOURCES: Same as for Table 1.

The study of Carruthers and Gwyer[11] indicated that the production of tea in Bangla Desh could be increased by expanding the acreage through reclamation of land similar to those adopted in India and other major tea-producing countries.

10 I.D. Carruthers and G.D. Gwyer, "Prospects for the Pakistan Tea Industry", *Pakistan Development Review*, Autumn 1968.
11 *Ibid.*

However, like jute, the excess supply of tea in the world market
was a major constraint in the expansion of tea exports from
Bangla Desh.   Even the exports to West Pakistan worth Rs 275
million in 1969-70 might also be difficult to sustain as
Ceylonese tea would be cheaper in West Pakistan.

The values of exports of other major export commodities
are shown in Table 9.   A distinguishing feature of the commodity composition of exports of Bangla Desh in recent years

TABLE 9

OTHER EXPORTS OF BANGLA DESH

(Rs millions)

Items	1958-59	1960-61	1964-65	1965-66	1966-67	1967-68	1968-69*
To Foreign Countries							
Hides and skins (raw)	28.5	28.6	20.0	16.8	2.6	N.A.	—
Spices	1.0	.5	3.6	4.9	5.3	N.A.	1.1
Cotton (raw)	4.9	4.2	4.8	1.9	1.8	14.5	.8
Hides and skins (tanned and leather)	—	3.7	12.4	24.8	33.9	N.A.	31.1
Cotton textiles	—	—	—	—	—	11.2	58.5
Other textiles	—	—	—	—	—	—	49.5
Paper and paper board	—	—	—	—	—	—	1.1
Chemicals	—	—	—	—	—	—	1.5
To West Pakistan							
Betelnuts	11.9	12.6	15.6	7.4	7.9	11.9	.5
Paper and paper board	28.6	39.0	85.9	78.9	76.3	91.0	55.4
Spices	—	—	—	—	18.0	10.6	.6
Leather	19.8	15.3	22.6	23.2	24.6	27.6	14.6
Matches	20.1	26.3	26.2	39.6	29.5	31.7	21.5

*Refers to data for 6 months.
SOURCES: *Statistical Digest of East Pakistan,* 1966; *Pakistan Economic Survey,*
1968-69, and *Monthly Statistical Bulletin,* March 1969.

(other than tea, fish, and jute goods) is the increasing share of manufactured products in the total value of exports. By and large, the exports of primary products like raw hides and skin, raw cotton, spices, and betelnuts are declining over the years while the exports of manufactured products like textiles-cotton and others, leather, matches, and paper and paper board are making rapid progress. In this context the great leap forward of exports of textiles, of all types, in the late sixties deserves particular attention. At present the production of cotton textiles in Bangla Desh depends largely on the imports of raw cotton from West Pakistan. Therefore, availability of raw cotton, particularly the imports of raw cotton, would have to be ensured for maintaining the tempo in the exports of cotton textiles. Another major obstacle would be the domestic absorption of cotton textiles in Bangla Desh. As Bangla Desh at present imports a significant amount of some varieties of cotton textiles from West Pakistan and other countries, the policy of restricting foreign imports and meeting the gap from domestic varieties may reduce the exportable surplus of cotton textiles in future.

The exports of matches and paper and paper board, which were hitherto exported mostly to West Pakistan, could now be diverted to other markets easily if West Pakistan restricts its imports of these commodities from Bangla Desh. The demand for them, particularly in India, is quite high. In general, the exports of paper and paper board, newsprint and timber and allied products could be stepped up by expanding the domestic output. The supply potential of these commodities is likely to be in excess of domestic demand and, hence, Bangla Desh may have some exportable surplus in these commodities. Further, if the proposed expansion of the fertilizer production capacity is materialized in the near future, fertilizer can also join the list of export items. An investment strategy of Bangla Desh suitably designed to tap these potentials can go a long way in promoting exports.

IV

The structure of imports of Bangla Desh has undergone some significant changes in recent years. Bangla Desh is now depending quite significantly on food imports. The major items of food imports are: rice, wheat, sugar and milk products.

TABLE 10

COMPOSITION OF FOREIGN IMPORTS OF BANGLA DESH

(Relative share in percentage)

Item		(1968-69) July December	Item		1961-62
Food—Total		21.0	Food		10.0
Wheat	14.0		Wheat	2	
Rice	3.5		Rice	3	
Sugar	1.0				
Milk product	1.0				
Coal, cokes and brickets		2.5	Coal, coke & brickets		3.5
Petroleum		1.5	Petroleum		4.0
Chemicals		9.0	Chemicals		4.5
Vegetable oil		5.0	Vegetable oil		2.0
Cement and lime		1.5	Cement & lime		2.5
Iron and steel		5.0	Iron & steel		7.0
Other minerals		10.0	Other minerals		8.5
Machinery and transport equipment		30.0	Machinery and transport equipment		25.0
Others		9.0	Others		32.0
		100			100

SOURCES: *Statistical Digest of East Pakistan,* 1966; and *Pakistan Economic Survey,* 1968-69.

About one fifth of all foreign imports of Bangla desh are now food items. This may put a severe strain on the foreign

TABLE 11

MAJOR FOREIGN IMPORTS OF BANGLA DESH

(*Rs million*)

Item	1958-59	1960-61	1964-65	1965-66	1966-67	1967-68	1968-69*
Rice	118	181	36	33	69	54	41
Wheat	22	39	49	102	160	198	177
Vegetable oil	5	13	14	17	40	65	55
Coal	42	30	49	30	34	41	24
Fuels	94	121	74	100	94	121	35
Iron and steel	8	34	337	238	299	199	105
Cement	6	11	52	31	18	20	12
Machinery and transport equipment	112	174	550	371	462	465	297
Chemicals and drugs	29	55	147	41	185	120	89

*Relates to six months of the period.

SOURCES: *Statistical Digest of East Pakistan*, 1966; and *Monthly Statistical Bulletin*, December 1968-March 1969.

exchange of Bangla Desh. The position in the recent years seems to be even worse.[12] The current food import requirement of Bangla Desh is likely to be somewhere in the range of Rs 350 - 500 million a year. At present about two-thirds of all imported rice comes from West Pakistan. In the case of wheat the share of West Pakistan in total imports is insignificant. The demand was largely met from PL 480 imports. The present wheat surplus of India can very well meet the wheat import requirement of Bangla Desh. Similar is the case

[12] *Pakistan Economic Survey*, 1970-71.

of sugar. The immediate import requirement of rice could be met by importing from Burma and Thailand which have some surplus.

The long-run objective in any case should be self-sufficiency in food, particularly in rice. The production and yields of rice in Bangla Desh have been stagnant in the sixties at about 10 million tons and 12 maunds per acre respectively. The impact of the green revolution and the new technology are yet to be felt in Bangla Desh. Therefore, any substantial increase

TABLE 12

MAJOR IMPORTS OF BANGLA DESH FROM WEST PAKISTAN

(Rs million)

Item	1958-59	1960-61	1964-65	1965-66	1966-67	1967-68	1968-69	1969-70
Rice	144	56	14	148	N.A.	94	18*	N.A.
Wheat	7	7	13	11	N.A.	18	10*	N.A.
Raw cotton	42	86	81	136	94	121	142	N.A.
Cotton yarn and thread	108	141	78	102	57	51	61	86
Cotton fabrics	74	145	184	183	221	195	217	242
Oil seeds	76	108	91	153	96	121	142	186
Raw tobacco	20	5	47	51	95	97	90	—
Manufac-tured tobacco	22	26	42	52	26	38	22	42
Cement	5	2	1	13	61	60	70	49
Machinery	22	23	40	54	53	67	66	86
Drugs	10	31	44	57	60	66	54	54
Manufac-tured metals	4	8	2	3	15	14	19	19

*Refers to the figure for 6 months of the period.

SOURCES: *Statistical Digest of East Pakistan*, 1966; *Pakistan Economic, Survey* 1968-69 and 1970-71; and *Monthly Bulletin of Statistics*, December 1968 and March 1969.

in the production of rice is possible only by increasing the acreage of rice and through the use of new-technology.[13] Since rice and jute are competitive crops, an increase in the acreage of rice would involve a decrease in the acreage of jute. With a secularly declining yield of jute, the production of jute is likely to suffer. In the short run, therefore, the drive for self sufficiency in rice may not be wholly compatible with the higher exports of raw jute and manufactured jute goods.

The embargo of trade with India affected some major import items like coal, machinery, cement, chemicals, drugs, and minerals. The values of imports of all these items in 1965-66 were lower by 20-40 per cent in comparison to those in 1964-65. India's shares in the total foreign imports of Bangla Desh in 1964-65 were roughly as follows: food—6 per cent, crude materials—10 per cent, minerals and fuels—10 per cent, chemicals and drugs—20 per cent, machinery—5 per cent, and manufactured goods—15 per cent. In many of these items West Pakistan was the real gainer as it enabled it to replace the cheaper Indian products by relatively costlier West Pakistani products into the Bangla Desh market. The value of foreign imports in most of these items picked up at a later stage largely due to the higher transportation costs of importing these items. Thus, while the value of imports and the index of the unit value of imports of Bangla Desh increased after 1965, the index of the quantum of imports had actually declined after that year.

In terms of broad groups, the relative shares of consumer

---

[13] The study of A.K.M.G. Rabbani and R.C. Repetto ("Foodgrains Availability, Money Supply and the Price Level in East Pakistan: Some Simple Econometrics on Short-Term Stabilization Policies", *Pakistan Development Review*, Summer 1968) suggests that the supply of rice is related to its price.

goods, industrial raw materials, and capital goods would be almost equal in the foreign imports of Bangla Desh. The relative share of consumer goods was in fact increasing over the years mainly due to the increasing dependence on the imports of food items. The composition of foreign imports of Bangla Desh is such that in the short-run there is very little possibility of import substitution as capacity in many of these items is almost non-existent. Of course, in the course of next few years the situation may change through industrialization.

The composition and the value of imports from West Pakistan may undergo some radical changes in the future. The value of imports from West Pakistan in recent years almost equals the value of all foreign imports. About 35 per cent of the imports from West Pakistan consists of raw materials and other primary products and the remaining 65 per cent are the manufactured products. The major items of raw materials imports from West Pakistan are raw cotton, raw tobacco, and oil seeds. The value of imports of raw cotton have increased by more than 200 per cent during the period 1958-1968. The value of imports of raw tobacco and oil seeds are also increasing rapidly in the last few years (see Table 12). The production and yields of raw cotton, raw tobacco, and oil seeds have been almost stagnant in Bangla Desh during the last two decades with some fluctuations. If Bangla Desh has to increase the production and exports of cotton textiles, the imports of raw cotton would have to increase. The imports of raw tobacco from West Pakistan can be replaced by raw tobacco from India at a cheaper transportation cost.

On the manufactured products side, there is likely to be a greater cut in the imports from West Pakistan. This may be partly due to the imports substitution of items like cement, paper and paper board, textiles, light machinery, and chemicals in which there is good supply potential in Bangla Desh. But to a greater extent, a relatively open competition among foreign products would itself restrict imports of many costly import items from West Pakistan which were hitherto protected under the federal commercial policy of former Pakistan. Thus, it is reasonable to expect a significant fall in the imports of manufactured tobacco, cotton textiles, chemicals and drugs, cement, limestone, and machinery from West Pakistan. The substitution of imports from West Pakistan is likely to reduce the costs of imports of Bangla Desh considerably.

V

The preceding analysis was concerned mainly with the existing trade pattern of Bangla Desh that it had inherited from the past and its likely pattern in the near future. The long-run trade pattern of independent Bangla Desh would be difficult to predict in the absence of a clear-cut idea regarding the aid flows, its quantum and also pattern. A significant feature that emerges from the analysis is that Bangla Desh now can have a trade pattern that is consistent with the principle of comparative cost advantage which has not been possible earlier due to the collonial commercial policy of the then federal government of Pakistan.

The annual values of exports and imports of Bangla Desh at the time of independence were roughly around Rs 2,700 million and Rs 3,800 million respectively. The value of exports may not change drastically in the immediate future. Some radical changes are, however, expected in the value and the composition of imports. In the first instance, the reopening of trade with India may reduce the costs of imports of some essential items like coal, cement, limestone, minerals, and machinery, etc., on the one hand, and may also increase the total volume of imports, on the other. Secondly, the removal of artificial restrictions on imports of Bangla Desh with unfavourable cost ratios for most of the imported items may increase the total volume of imports. Finally, the process of industrialization itself will make rapid increase in the imports of industrial raw materials and capital goods. The combined effect of all these factors may push the value of imports substantially higher in comparison with the level of imports in the pre-Independence period.

The previous analysis showed that there may be conflicts between the short and the long run trade objectives of Bangla Desh. Jute is an area where such conflicts are likely to occur. The short-run objective of exporting raw jute to India to pay for increasing import requirements may conflict with its long-run interest of promoting the exports of manufactured jute goods. Here, a clear-cut policy of cooperation between Bangla Desh and India in the world jute market is essential to protect the interests of both the countries, particularly in view of the fact that the world demand is stagnating. A considerable effort will also have to be made to have the twin objectives of promoting the production of both rice and raw jute through green revolution. Otherwise, due to the production substitutability of rice and jute, the increase in the foreign exchange earnings through increased production and exports of jute goods would be compensated by the loss of foreign exchange from the import of rice.

To sum up, Bangla Desh will inherit a colonial trade pattern from East Pakistan, with a heavy dependence on traditional items for exports and consumer goods for imports. For a short period Bangla Desh may not face any serious balance of trade problem. However, industrialization may alter this pattern and Bangla Desh is likely to face an acute deficit balance of trade problem unless it is able to find some new commodities for export and also able to cut drastically its food and other non-essential consumer goods import.

A. M. KHUSRO

INDIA-BANGLA DESH TRADE AND INVESTMENT PROSPECTS

IF BANGLA DESH had been a region with very meagre natural endowments and West Pakistan had very substantial endowments, one could have condoned the differences in the levels of investment, levels of living, and rates of economic growth. It is well-known that any attempt to force equality between two *very differently endowed* regions is bound to compromise the overall rate of economic growth. Differences in economic levels and growth rates are bound to persist under those circumstances of vastly different endowments.

But this was not necessarily the case between West Pakistan and East Pakistan of the last 24 years. East Pakistan was not a badly endowed region and there was no good reason why through economic planning and investment, and through other instruments of policy a high level and rate of economic growth, as high or nearly as high as in West Pakistan, could not have been achieved. No doubt, in the short period, particularly during its Second Five-Year Plan (1959-1964), Pakistan did achieve a reasonably high rate of growth at the cost of compromising balanced regional development of her two regions. But in the longer run, the relative under-development of the eastern region was destined to slow down Pakistan's overall rate, apart from causing the economic discontent and the resultant political discontent which has finally led to the demand for an independent Bangla Desh, now successfully achieved.

There is overwhelming evidence now available to show that the investment pattern, the export-import set up, the fiscal instruments and nearly everything else was so fashioned as to keep East Pakistan in a permanent state of relative poverty. Its industrial potential was not properly developed and, in fact, it was used as a market for consumer goods produced in West Pakistan; its foreign exchange earnings were deflected very considerably for use in West Pakistan; its entrepreneurial talent did not fully emerge; and its growth rate at the best of times (over any 5-year period) did not exceed 4 per cent, when West Pakistan in the same period had a growth rate of 7 per cent.

Prospects of Trade

What are some of the basic principles that ought to be followed in India's trade with Bangla Desh and in helping Bangla Desh with the expansion of her investment programme? Economic relations between Bangla Desh and India cannot be organized on the basis of sentiment; they could only be organized on considerations of hard realism. As wisdom would have it, in the long-run Bangla Desh will have no permanent enemies; it will have no permanent friends; it will, like India or any other country, have only permanent interests. The basic point to note about Indo-Bangla trade is that before 1947 the area that is now Bangla Desh and the area that is India had the benefits of internal trade with each other. After 1947, when these areas became areas of international trade, that trade virtually stopped. It stopped completely after 1965, except, perhaps, for its illicit component. The major consequence of that stoppage was that losses from non-trading occurred in both countries and the magnitude of these losses can be shown to be very large. The losses from non-trading were large because before partition, East Bengal and India had a much greater complementarity in production and trade than the complementarity that existed, say, between East Punjab and West Punjab. The jute economies, the rice economies and the tea economies of the east were much more integrated and complementary than the wheat economy of the Punjab. After partition, a lot of autarkic development occurred on both sides, new interests arose in production and trade, and East Bengal and East India behaved as though they were unaware of the existence of each other.

Now with an independent Bangla Desh the largest single impact on Bangla Desh and India would be that gains from trade will replace the losses from non-trading, whatever the pattern and the commodity composition of trade. Whether the balance of trade between India and Bangla Desh is in balance or out of balance, gains from trade will be immense.

The general principles which can be recommended in Indo-Bangla Desh trade would appear to be as follows:

(a) Whatever East Bengal was selling to the rest of India before partition, and lost after 1947, can be resumed if comparative advantage still lies that way and subject to some important qualifications.

(b) What Bangla Desh was exporting to the rest of the world, India should encourage its continuation and further expansion, so that the foreign exchange earnings of Bangla Desh get enhanced.

(c) Whatever Bangla Desh was selling to West Pakistan,

we should try and buy from her, provided we have shortages of those items—and there are several items which come under this category.

(d) Whatever East Bengal was importing from the rest of India in the pre-partition days could now be resumed, provided that the comparative advantages still lie in this direction.

(e) Whatever Bangla Desh was importing from the rest of the world, India can now supply as many of those items as possible, in so far as India's productive capabilities have altered substantially in the last 24 years and the transport cost from India to Bangla Desh will be considerably less than the cost from other areas of the world.

(f) Whatever Bangla Desh was importing from West Pakistan, India should think twice before selling that— in particular, those manufactured consumer goods which Bangla Desh can itself manufacture, given an opportunity.

These principles can be established on the basis of hard economic reasoning and good theory and can be shown to be healthy principles in the long-run. These principles can be illustrated.

Bangla Desh always had capabilities in raw jute exports and has further developed capabilities in jute manufacture exports to the rest of the world. This important source of foreign exchange should obviously not be compromised through Indian intervention. On the other hand, provided a reasonable price offer is made by India, Bangla Desh could produce raw jute over and above her manufacturing requirements and sell to India for India's jute manufacture. As for sales of manufactured jute goods to the rest of the world, the two countries must enter into an agreement which prevents head-long competition. This may well take the form of a 'jute community'. Bangla Desh tea exports had declined sharply in recent years, as they had been deflected into the West Pakistani market. These exports to the rest of the world will now be resumed and will begin to compete with India's exports. Here, too, it is important that the two countries have a mutual agreement for world sales. Until West Pakistan, some time later, hopefully, resumes import of tea from India and Bangla Desh, these countries could sell tea to third countries, who would then sell to Pakistan.

Bangla Desh was selling to West Pakistan betelnuts, spices, wood and timber, among primary goods, and tea, jute goods, paper and paper board, matches and leather among manu-factured or processed goods. Now that these sales will be impossible, at any rate for some time, we could take over their supplies of betelnuts, spices, wood and timber, paper and paper board, and newsprint and, in fact, buy in much larger quantities than they were supplying to West Pakistan, thereby giving an impetus for the further expansion of their export industries. We will, of course, not be able to buy much tea or jute goods from Bangla Desh. Nor, perhaps, their matches and leather.

On the side of Bangla Desh imports, several items which West Pakistan was selling to the East could now be sold by us. In the short period, of course, we could sell everything on the side of manufactured consumer goods of which we do not have serious shortages. But in the medium and the longer run, we should be very chary of exporting to Bangla Desh all the items which Bangla Desh was getting from

West Pakistan. Of course, we could sell machinery, drugs and medicine, metals, rubber goods and tobacco. We cannot sell oil seeds and raw cotton, of which we have shortages. But the basic point is that there are many lines of production which Bangla Desh, given a chance, could operate itself, in the nature of foot-loose industries and consumer-goods industries, giving her people a lot more employment as well as the benefit of inexpensive local production. These lines were not encouraged by West Pakistan, the idea being to provide outlets for her own production. What India can do now is to help develop Bangla Desh capacities in these lines by selling them not the final manufactured goods, but (a) the raw materials, and (b) the equipment and machinery to promote the manufacture of those goods, e.g., cotton textiles, cigarettes and tobacco products, paper and paper board and vegetable oils. The cement industry of Bangla Desh could, of course, get its equipment as well as its limestone supplies from India. In other words, in the line of consumer goods we should sell to Bangla Desh not everything which West Pakistan sold, but only such items as Bangla Desh does not have the potential to produce and for which we have the capacity and surplus. On the other hand, the development of new lines of consumer goods in Bangla Desh need not stand in the way of our trade, as we can still supply the equipment and the intermediate goods, in particular, coal, petroleum and limestone for the manufacture of those goods. If Bangla Desh has a power grid and if we have one, linkages for power supply can bring an enormous benefit to both areas and Indian supplies of low grade coal can, perhaps, go a long way in the achievement of this ambition.

Prospects of Investment

Trade will, no doubt, evolve itself apart from being promoted. But the real rub is likely to come in the field of investment. India's experiences with American investment in this country on the receiving side and with Indian investment in Nepal on the giving side, and the experience with private Indian investment in many African countries provides enough lessons about how not to deal in the field of investment. This is obviously an area of great touchiness and ample care would be necessary. Here some general principles will be as follows:

Bangla Desh has a good number of very competent economists and planners, who should help the Government with adequate planning and targeting in different lines of reconstruction and expansion. Once investment targets are determined, and once Bangla Desh is generally recognized, investment flows from international organizations will no doubt occur.

As for lines of credit and help from India, it would be important to discourage private sources. Of course, matters will depend on the policies adopted by the Bangla Desh Government itself, which may or may not encourage private foreign investment. But no initiative needs to be taken from this country in respect of private sources. Government to Government investment can of course be discussed. However, it is important not to allow the usual criticisms to emerge about foreign technicians demanding extraordinarily high salaries compared with local scales, keeping the know-how to themselves rather than part with it, and remitting large and unacceptable amounts of profit to their respective countries. It would seem that civil servants and do-gooders are the worst categories, and scientists and intellectuals perhaps the best categories of persons to be sent to Bangla Desh. With scores of scientific laboratories and defence science laboratories, India is in a goood position to share scientific know-how with Bangla Desh scientists and technologists. It is best that the Government of Bangla Desh should itself decide what technology to buy from India, which has some achievements in new technological lines, what capital goods to purchase on commercial terms, what lines of credit to ask for, what technicians to hire and what consultancies to demand. But the entire responsibility for wrong choices of techniques, for placing the wrong orders, and for hiring the wrong people should be of those who buy and hire these.

The other alternative would be to make a contract with India for the setting up of a particular project of a given technology, with all the details of consultancy and service worked out and the durations and other terms of the contract clearly specified, so that, once the job is done, the foreigners can quit. Basically, investment from abroad in Bangla Desh should be entirely according to the wish of the Government and the people of Bangla Desh, provided supplies exist from India and other countries.

ARJUN SENGUPTA

ECONOMIC RECONSTRUCTION OF BANGLA DESH: IMMEDIATE PERSPECTIVE*

THE VICTORY OF the liberation movement in Bangla Desh is going to be the beginning of another great struggle for the rebuilding of *Sonar Bangla*.

The people of Bangla Desh are among the poorest in the world, overwhelmingly dependent on backward agriculture. One of the flattest pieces of alluvial land in the world criss-crossed by mighty rivers and innumerable rivulets, this country could have become the granary of the entire subcontinent. But its history was different, and now the time has come to remake that history.

It is also a great moment for us, the people of India. Almost as poor as the people of Bangla Desh, we have joined hands with them—first in their struggle for liberation from tyranny, and then in their great struggle for reconstruction. The victory in the war of liberation was not easy, but the fight for economic reconstruction and development is bound to be much more difficult. Here, in the sphere, one cannot wait for any miracle. Our potential is limited, and our ability to help is

---

*Published in *Mainstream*, 25 December 1971, and 1 January 1972.

very small. And it is going to be a long and arduous process of concerted efforts by the people of Bangla Desh, organized by their Government, planned and executed by their planners and administrators.

Our relations with them can be neither of aid-givers nor of advisers. These have to be based on mutual help and benefits of trade and economic relations. Chauvinism has to be ruled out, not only because it is inexpedient in both the long and the short-run perspectives but also because it would be ridiculously out of proportion with our ability.

But we cannot shirk our responsibility either. We have chosen to be partners with the people of Bangla Desh in the process of remaking their destiny. After nine months of wanton rampage by the occupation forces of Pakistan and a devastating war, the base from which the process of remaking will start is almost in shambles. There are many areas where we can be of no help, but there are some fields where we can be useful, and some others where our joint efforts could yield immense benefits. We cannot avoid responding to their great endeavour for reconstruction with equal efforts on our part.

The relationship between these two countries is going to evolve through time and understanding of each other's problems. This note is a modest attempt to help that process of understanding by trying to give a very tentative picture of the immediate economic problems of reconstruction of Bangla Desh. The information regarding the economy of Bangla Desh is very limited. After 1968, very little literature about Pakistan's economy has come to India. Within a short period we should have more precise information about the economic conditions of Bangla Desh. Many of the statements we shall be making here may, therefore, have to be revised. Yet a beginning has to be made, and this note is written in that spirit.

The most immediate problem in Bangla Desh will be to ensure adequate food supply to the people, and this depends on both the availability of foodgrains and the distribution of whatever that is available. Bangla Desh, that was East Bengal, has been a food deficit state. In recent times, more than a million tons of foodgrains had to be imported every year. Although the population is predominantly rice-eating, imports to meet their food deficit were largely of wheat, of the order of seven to eight lakh tons from West Pakistan and from other countries. In spite of that, food consumption in East Bengal during the last three years hardly exceeded 15 to 16 ounces a day per person.

When the civil war broke out in March this year, there was widespread speculation that East Bengal was going to face a severe famine. There was a sharp fall in rice production in the preceding major *aman* (winter) crop due to flood and cyclone. An immediate result of the civil war was serious dislocation of the transport system and the channels of distribution. The Government of Pakistan made an estimate of two million tons of food deficit in East Bengal in 1971-72. A World Bank report of July 1971 stated that two million tons of foodgrains would have to be imported betweeen July and December 1971 to maintain a daily supply of 5.4 ounces per person, and a reasonable level of stocks. But as time went on, there was not much sign of widespread famine, though there were some pockets of acute scarcity, particularly in the urban and food deficit areas.

There were several reasons for this. First, and probably the most important, reason was the huge exodus of people

from East Bengal as if famine was sought to be exported from
East Pakistan to India. This potentially large saving on food
consumption was not taken into account in earlier predictions
of famine, and this saving comes conveniently to Pakistan
in the lean season of food production. The exact quantum
of this saving is difficult to calculate. It would depend upon
the rate of flow of the refugees, their composition in terms of
age, occupation and income group, and the areas from which
they came, whether they were surplus or deficit. A rough
calculation on the basis of assumptions indicated that the
refugees were evenly drawn from all the areas, that their per
capita consumption was 15 ounces a day, and that, after an
initial spurt of exodus leading to a saving of two million man-
mouths in April, the rate of flow was even at one million
a month ending with a full nine million man-mouth saving in
November, would give a figure at more than 550,000 tons
foodgrains saved on this account. The actual figure might be
much higher if the flow of refugees was large in the initial
months, and if, as is reported, they came mostly from the surplus
border districts such as Dinajpur, Rangpur, Rajshahi, Bogra
and Jessore, as the per capita consumption there should be
higher than the average for the whole province.

Lower Consumption

Secondly, there are difinite indications that the per capita
consumption of those who stayed back actually fell. All reports
suggest that there was a drastic fall of purchasing power in
the hands of people due to the disruption of the rural works
programmes and other economic activities. Besides, in
distress conditions, people are accustomed to curtailing their

consumption and sharing out with others in the family and kinship groups whatever they have. In 1966-67 there was a sharp fall in food production and availability in East Bengal, but there was no outbreak of famine in open form, as people adjusted themselves to a level of per capita consumption of about 13.8 ounces a day, about two ounces less than in previous years. If a similar adjustment occurred this year, the pressure from the demand side on foodgrains was relaxed.

Thirdly, in March this year, the Government had already a stock of about 770,000 tons of foodgrains from the very large imports of foodgrains of the previous year. The Government of Pakistan had also drawn up a schedule of imports of food-grains between May and October from the USA, China, Japan and West Pakistan amounting to about 770,000 tons. How much of these imports could actually be brought in is not known. But to the extent some imports were effected and the Government stocks were allowed to be replenished, they must have relieved the food shortage to some extent, especially in urban areas where the government distribution shops operated.

Furthermore, this year the *boro* (spring) crop turned out to be very good, on the trend of last few years. The civil war broke out around the harvesting time and although there was some loss and damage of crop, it is doubtful that harvesting of ripe crop was very much disrupted, and the official estimate of 2.2 million tons of production may not be an over-estimate. The *aus* (summer) crop production still continues more or less in the traditional style of cultivation without much use of fertilizers, and its increase in recent years was mostly due

to expanding acreage. The economic disturbances affecting
fertilizer supply could not affect cultivation much, and the
rise in the price of rice in relation to jute brought more land
under this crop. The major impact of large-scale migration
of farmers has been mostly in the delay of planting in a
largely over-populated state like East Bengal. This delay
would have an effect on the major winter crop, *aman*, where
planting in many areas was also delayed leading to a definite
fall in productivity. But the output of *aus* crop was not much
affected and a USAID estimate of 2.47 million tons might
be somewhat conservative.

Disconcerting Aspect

Although all these factors might possibly explain why a famine
in an open form did not break out in East Bengal during the
occupation regime, they also very clearly lead to another
conclusion which is very disconcerting for the new Bangla
Desh Government in its immediate programme of reconstruction. In the beginning of December, there must have
been very little stock of foodgrains left in Bangla Desh. If
we take the combined output of the *boro* and the *aus* crops of
4.67 million tons and deduct the usual 10 per cent as wastage,
seed, etc, and also take, very liberally, 1.4 million tons
as the net government stock (630,000 tons stock as the end
of March official figure plus 770,000 tons of imports between
April and October) we get a total availability figure of
5.6 million tons. This would have been hardly sufficient
to maintain 59 to 60 million people on the average for eight
months between April and November at a rate of consumption
of only 14 ounces per day per person. The highest estimate

of the refugee influx in India was 10 million in December which would have left at least 65 million people still in East Bengal, and in earlier months the population was sustained by a steady depletion of whatever privately held stock that was available in East Bengal from the output of foodgrains before March 1971. The size of such stocks was usually not very large, and it must have been even smaller than the usual because of the poor *aman* crop of the last year. So, the actual stock of foodgrains with the people of Bangla Desh at the beginning of December must have been really negligible.

The situation would have been extremely critical for the Bangla Desh Government had it not been for the fact that liberation came at the time when the major *aman* crop was being harvested. We do not as yet have much information about the actual size of this crop. Reports up to about November suggest that the crop this year was quite good. In recent years, except for the 1970 floods, *aman* production in East Bengal registered 10 to 11 per cent rate of growth, and that also mostly due to the rise in productivity as changes in acreage have been rather small. The size of the 1969 bumper crop was 6.95 million tons. Although weather conditions were good, there are reasons to believe that the size of the crop this year should be smaller.

First, it is reasonable to assume that the acreage under *aman* has fallen quite substantially this year. During the past decade, practically no trend was observed in *aman* acreage which ranged between 14.1 and 15.1 million acres. Districts where large *aman* crops are normally raised are mostly in border areas like Mymensingh, Sylhet, Rangpur, Khulna, Comilla, Rajshahi and Dinajpur. These were the areas worst affected by the exodus of farming population. Since these were the main theatres of the liberation war in the final stage, even if the crops were raised their harvesting must have been substantially damaged leading to an effective loss of acreage. Barisal is also another important *aman* producing district, but it was badly affected by the last year's cyclone, and the latest reports indicated that only a small fraction of the loss of implements and livestock had been restored.

Furthermore, a large part—usually 25 to 35 per cent— of the *aman* acreage follows *aus* production and since *aus* was later this year than usual, this must have had some effect on the production of *aman* in spite of the fact that the weather was not very dry towards the end of the season.

Crucial Problem

In addition, there was the impact of severe dislocation of the channels of distribution of fertilizers and pesticides. The effect of the short supply of fertilizers and pesticides must have been felt very acutely in the HYV Programmes. In the last couple of years, IR-20 had been successfully introduced during the *aman* season. Net acreage under IR-20 in the *aman* season of 1970, after allowances for floods, was estimated at 166,500 acres, with a rise in yield by about 25 to 50 per cent. The Government of Pakistan had a revised programme of bringing about one million acres under this high-yielding variety of seeds this year, 1971. But the production here is highly susceptible to timely supply of seeds, fertilizers and pesticides. Disruption of the transport system and the agricultural credit system as have been described in the reports of the World Bank and the USAID as also in the newspapers could not have ensured the required amount and rate of supply of these inputs. In addition to all this, the entire process of *aman* planting lagged behind the schedule. For HYV, the recommended time of transplanting is usually mid-July, which would require seedling to have gone into nurseries by mid-June. A World Bank report of mid-July speaks of very little preparation of fields or nursery-beds for this purpose.

With all these considerations in mind, it seems reasonable to assume that the acreage under *aman* this year was about 13 million acres—ten per cent below the average of the last few years—with about half a million acres successfully brought under IR-20. Assuming a yield of 12 maunds per acre under local variety—the average of the yields between 1960 and 1966—and a yield of 20 maunds per acre under IR-20, one gets an estimate of 5.9 to 6 million tons of output of the last *aman* crop in Bangla Desh. Deducting 10 per cent for wastage seeds, etc. this would leave about 5.5 million tons of rice for consumption.

If all the foodgrains could have been evenly distributed it would have maintained a population of 7.5 million at 15.5 ounces a day per person for a period of more than five months till the next *boro* crop was harvested.

Serious Problems

Here comes the crucial problem of management, the successful solution of which would depend very much on the skill and organization of the Government, their political support and local initiative.

Under normal conditions, only about 10 per cent of the total food output in East Bengal used to be disposed of through commercial channels of trade. Most of the remaining output used to be either absorbed by the producers or sold in areas near the place of production. In the next few months, if the usual forces are relied upon, this commercial flow should be expected to be much smaller. First, the producer's own demand for food would be higher than in normal times, for they would try to replenish their depleted private stocks. Secondly, the transport bottlenecks, unless cleared, would increase sharply the cost of such commercial flows. And, thirdly, the reduced economic activity of the last nine months and the virtual stoppage of rural works programme have left very little purchasing power with the people to buy foodgrains at commercial prices.

It is important to realize the significance of this point. About 10 million refugees in India from Bangla Desh are presently in the process of returning home. If they have to be sustained on the marketed surplus of foodgrains, the problems that would be created would be extremely serious. They will add to the already large number of people who have been displaced from their home and occupation and escaped from tyranny by migrating to different parts of the country. There is also a large population, almost pamperized through lack of jobs, reduced economic activity and disruption of work programmes, and have survived on the borderline of hunger with a very low per capita consumption during the last nine months. As works programmes are started again, economic activities revived and purchasing power created, all the repressed demand would come out in the open. In the face of this gigantic problem, the mere existence of sufficient foodgrains for a few months with the producers, could hardly be a source of comfort.

It is obvious that the only way to tackle such a problem is to introduce rationing immediately throughout Bangla Desh coupled with a big programme of procurement of foodgrains from the farmers. Organizationally, this is going to be a very difficult job. In the scarcity conditions, price incentives may not yield much of procurement, and the Government may have to depend on non-price measures like taxes and levies. Furthermore, the sources of a rationing system would depend very much upon the speed with which the internal transport system is brought to its normal level of operation, facilitating the movement of grains from relatively surplus to deficit areas.

During the last few years, the Food Department of the then East Pakistan Government was running fair-price ration shops in most of the urban areas. In normal years their offtake in the lean months had been around 140,000 to 144,000 tons a month. This year, the Government estimated that the rate of offtake should have been of the order of 175,000 tons. The grains distributed by the Government were almost entirely drawn from imports. Between July and October this year, the scheduled imports into East Bengal averaged at 160,000 tons a month, and the Government proposed to import 200,000 tons of foodgrains in each month subsequent to october 1971.

Heavy Imports

The total requirement of foodgrains for the rationing system in Bangla Desh along the lines proposed above should be much higher than for the usual Food Department stores during the last couple of years. The Food Department supplies were supplementary to the normal trade through commercial channels, when the people and the Government already had some reasonable stocks. As has been already noted, the commercial channels have very little prospect of effective operation in Bangla Desh in the near future. The Government rationing programme will have to be much more comprehensive and must cover very large sections of the population. This will have to be, under the necessity of the circumstances, very largely a substitute for commercial distributive channels. For that the Government of Bangla Desh will have to procure food from the internal market, but, in spite of that, very large imports of foodgrains would become necessary.

A simple calculation will show the magnitude of the problem. An offtake of 200,000 tons of foodgrains per month from the government shops would maintain only about 15 million people at 15.5 ounces a day per person. For five months from January to May, this would amount to a total supply of one million tons. If the Government wants to build up a reserve stock of a minimum of 500,000 tons, the total requirement of foodgrains for the Government rationing system for the next five months will be 1.5 million tons. Of our estimated net production of *aman* crops of 5.5 million tons, suppose as much as five million tons are left with the people by 1 January 1972, then, even if the Government procured 10 per cent of this—a figure that would be very difficult to reach as that is the usual rate of marketed surplus in normal years—there will still remain a gap of one million tons which will have to be met by imports on an average of 200,000 tons a month.

The question that remains to be discussed is whether the transport system of Bangla Desh will be able to absorb inputs of this order and distribute them internally to the right places in required amounts. The major food deficit areas in Bangla Desh are Dacca, Mymensingh and Comilla where about 33 per cent of the population lives. In Barisal and Faridpur, locally produced rice normally flows both to Dacca and the major towns and cities which are deficit. Food from other relatively surplus districts moves to the central areas through commercial channels by rails and roads. From the ports, food can move to Dacca by fairly large water transport, or by trunk road. Mymensingh is further up-country and can be served by water with smaller carriers taking circuitous routes or by metre-gauge rail-road.

Information is not yet available on the basis of which one can say even approximately how these transport media will be operating. During the nine months of occupation by the Pakistan army and the struggle of the Mukti Bahini, and finally during the decisive stage of the war, numerous bridges, culverts, signalling posts, and rails have been damaged or destroyed. A comprehensive assessment of these damages will have to be made before an optimal routing system can be devised to solve the immediate problems of transportation. We do not yet know also how much damage has been done to the Chittagong port, what the condition of its jetty, grain silo, port-sheds and warehouses is. Together they determine how much imports can be handled in Chittagong, given the rates of clearance by rail, road and water. During 1969-70, nearly 3.3 million tons of import cargo was cleared in Chittagong, of which 1.46 million tons was foodgrains. This was over 20 per cent higher than the average of 2.73 million tons of the preceding three years. Most of this increase in clearance was by water; the rate of transport by water that year was almost five times that of the preceding years.

This shows that water transport has a large potential of absorbing a heavy additional demand for transportation. The rate of such absorption would depend on the number and size of barges, coasters, vessels, etc., that might be available. The supply of such vessels can be increased rather quickly, which enhances the importance of using the potential of water transport to meet the immediate problems of food distribution.

II

The immediate challenge that the new Government in Bangla Desh will have to face is the problem of ensuring adequate supply of foodgrains to its impoverished population as discussed in the earlier part of this paper.

We have seen that the problem is difficult, but not beyond solution. And the degree of success in solving this problem will be a direct function of the organizing ability of the popular government—how fast it can restore the transport network to normalcy, how efficiently it can devise a rationing system and how effectively it can mobilize a system of foodgrains procurement.

The test of the organizational efficiency will also be seen in other fields of economic activity. The work of reconstruction will have to be started immediately in agriculture, industry, trade and commerce. During the nine months of the military occupation, production activities in all these fields were severely disrupted. Reports of the World Bank, the USAID, foreign correspondents, the refugees, and whatever other sources that are available, indicate a picture that is disorganized, chaotic, and suffering from extreme uncertainty and lack of confidence. The major factors that were identified as responsible for this state of affairs should not be operative any more now that the country is liberated. But still it will take time and organization to normalize the situation.

For example, the flight of labour, especially skilled and experienced, brought many of the activities to a grinding halt. Now, as all these labourers start returning, these activities can be started again, but still there will remain the problem of phasing and adjustment. In agriculture, this problem might assume very serious dimensions. In an over-populated, land-scarce country like Bangla Desh, the vacuum created by the exodus of the people from the farms must have already been filled to a substantial extent by others who have engaged in production activities during occupation period and have raised about two crops. It will be a mammoth job to absorb the return of refugees in the lands they tilled and cultivated before they left.

The flight of the refugees together with the uncertainties generated by the military regime had their worst impact on trade and commerce. A World Bank report recorded the destruction of the town and village markets, and stocks, with the disappearance of numerous small, retail and wholesale traders, and even for those who remained, there was a severe disruption of trading links due to the drying up of credit facilities. As the outstanding commitments were seldom settled, creditors were reluctant to extend their operation, and the link between importers, manufacturers, distributors and retailers almost broke down. Similar disruption was there of the commercial links between jute farmers, intermediate markets jute manufacturers and jute shippers.

The lack of confidence was most reflected in the banking operation. The deposit base of the banks in East Bengal shrank very rapidly and the West Pakistani banks were limiting their operations to the local deposit base. In spite of the Government's substantial liberalization of the rediscounting facilities to the banks operating in East Bengal, to relieve their liquidity problem, the banks were not found willing to provide much credit.

As the refugees start coming back, and traders try to begin their operation, the Government is sure to face a rather difficult problem. In the scarcity condition of the post-war economy, and as the Government starts generating purchasing power through its programmes of reconstruction, there will be very large scope for profiteering by the traders at all levels. Indeed, if the traditional trade channels are fully restored, private traders can, by raising their trade margins, create artificial scarcities, frustrating the speedy implementation of the reconstruction plans. But taking over the entire private trade throughout the state may not be a feasible solution in the present state of the economy and administration.

This will be particularly significant in the case of jute, where the operation of trading links has so much effect on the output and productivity of a major economic activity. It will be disastrous to leave this operation unrestricted in the hands of private traders, for jute is a major pillar of the Bangla Desh economy, and its output, productivity and expansion will have to be strictly supervised. On the other hand, this whole operation is so diversified and so sensitive to price movements that a central bureaucratic machinery cannot hope to tackle all the problems.

Bank Nationalization Inevitable

All these would require a very skilful combination of strict social control with decentralized, private initiative and decision-making. In the case of banking, nationalization is almost inevitable, with most of the banks being owned by West Pakistanis or foreigners and with the necessity that their operations be guided not by commercial but by social profitability, especially in the transitional period. But just a nationalization of the banks will not be enough. The whole banking structure will have to be rebuilt, the entire method of operation will have to be changed, the norms of behaviour will have to be geared to activities that have long-run social benefits.

Banking finance will be necessary not only for trade and commerce but also for other economic activities like industrial production and farming operations, and a careful reorganization of the banking system to provide that finance efficiently would require much more than nationalization.

It is obvious that such a restructuring of banking and commerce is a time-consuming process. But unfortunately the Government in Bangla Desh has very little time to lose as the revitalization of a large part of the production system now crucially depends on finance and ready availability of credit. In agriculture, all the efforts will have to be directed immediately to the production of food crop, particularly for the next *boro* season. This is the time for the planting of the crop that will be harvested in April-May 1972. The production of this crop has rapidly expanded in recent years due to modernization of farming techniques and increasing acreage brought

under improved seeds of IR-8 variety.   Indeed, if the trend in
its production of the last few years is maintained, we could
expect a 2.5 million ton output of rice from this crop this
year.   Furthermore, most of its production occurs in the
deficit districts like Mymensingh, Dacca and Comilla,
besides Sylhet and Chittagong.   All energy has to be devoted
to make this crop a success.

The *boro* crop is almost entirely dependent on mechanical
irrigation and must receive much heavier application of
fertilizers and pesticides than *aman* or *aus* to maintain a high
average yield per acre.   In Bangla Desh, irrigation for this crop
is done mostly by low-lift pumps and tubewells whose introduction has expanded at a very rapid rate in the last few
years.   Many of these pumps have been damaged due to
poor maintenance and lack of repair and spare-part, and the
absence of trained mechanics.   Compensating for all these
damages plus a substantial additional installation of pumps
to expand acreage under this crop would call for a large programme of purchase and distribution of these pumps in the
country.

Even if this programme of installation of pumps is implemented, the success of this crop would depend on how much
fertilizer and pesticide can be applied by the farmers in time
during the season.   And this in turn would depend most on
the purchasing power of the farmer.   Even though in East
Bengal fertilizers used to be subsidised at 60 per cent of the
CIF price, it remained the most expensive input to the farmer.
Usually, the farmer had to borrow heavily to finance this
purchase.

The other major problem will be that of pesticides where
in spite of sizable stocks of these materials being available,

their distribution will face difficulties. Besides the bottlenecks of transportation there will be shortage of sprayers either because they are damaged or because of the scarcity of petrol. Granular pesticides that do not require mechanical sprayers, and can be used for certain parts, if water depth can be controlled, are not available in large quantity and are also fairly expensive.

In any case, since the *boro* crop is dependent on inputs, and the application of inputs is dependent on the purchasing power of the farmers, the success of this crop is crucially related to the rate and the speed with which the supply of agricultural credit is expanded. The operation of the traditional money-lenders will be exploitation and will act as a brake on the productive system. On the other hand, the revival of co-operative agricultural credit system, in the present state of affairs, will be invariably linked to the expansion of the banking system in the rural areas.

Most Expensive Input

In the case of jute, a rupture in the trade-credit nexus has a very damaging effect on the production of raw jute. If bottlenecks develop in the export market, or the manufacturers do not wish to build up additional stocks, advances made by traders to the farmers tend to dry up. The cultivation of jute is more costly than of rice, and, besides the cost of fertilizers, there are expenses for weeding and other operations and also for more labour input. If finance and credit are scarce, the traders often use their monopoly power of the buyer and depress the prices that the farmers receive. A fall in the price of jute in relation to rice almost invariably leads to a shift of acreage away from jute to rice, which might reduce the output of jute substantially in that very same year. It will be necessary for the Bangla Desh Government to face this problem immediately as jute is its principal foreign exchange earner. It will have to set a minimum price for jute, after an assessment of the jute-rice price relations, and provide enough purchasing power to the farmer through the credit system, so that the acreage remaining under jute is effectively cultivated.

In the manufacturing sector also, the immediate task will be to get the production activities moving. Quite a number of the manufacturing units will fall naturally in the hands of the Government as they were owned by West Pakistanis. Some others might have to be taken over as the private owners may not have the capacity to revitalize them with efficiency. But the need of the hour is the revival of production and all changes in the ownership and structure of industries will have to be geared to this immediate necessity.

Prior to the war, physical destruction or damage to plants and equipment had not been large. The Mukti Bahini had no interest in destroying the productive assets of Bangla Desh. Some jute warehouses and tea-chest factories in Chittagong, a couple of tea factories in Sylhet, a paper mill at Tangi and some saw mills, brick kilns and hand-looms around Narsingdi and in north-west Bangla Desh were practically all that were burnt down or damaged. Several cases have been reported of damage to machinery and equipment caused by faulty maintenance. Many electric metres have burnt out by voltage fluctuations, several plants were corroded and were lying with unrepaired breakages. The rayon plant at Karnafuli Paper Mill was severely damaged by sulphuric acid left in the system. The fertilizer plant at Ghorasal, with a capacity of 340,000 tons of urea per year was improperly shut down and was lying badly corroded.

The toll of the final war is not yet known. The retreating army of Pakistan followed a scortched-earth policy which must have left its stamp behind in the destruction of some plants and equipment. Obviously, a massive job of repairs will have to be started to restore all the machinery and equipment to their normal level of operation. But the crucial factor responsible for a virtual collapse of manufacturing activity during the military occupation of the last nine months was the lack of finance and liquidity due to loss of sales and transport bottlenecks. Large stocks of finished goods accumulated at different factory sites leading to a slowing down of production. The Chhatak Cement and Fenchuganj Fertilizer factories have nearly exhausted their storage capacities. Several sugar mills were left with large unsold stocks. Many firms have been forced to operate at cumulative losses with reduced level of production and restricted sales and the negative cash flows, while disruption of short-term credit facilities led to non-payment of wages and other expenses and a severe neglect of maintenance and other normal activities.

A programme of revival of production here has to be based on careful organization and planning with attention to details and specific requirements of different production units. And, above all, finance has to be provided to manufacturing units, whether they are operated in the private or the public sector. Lifting the stocks and their sales will only partially solve the problem of liquidity and cash flows. Requirements of funds to carry out the repairs and to bring the production system to a state where the units can be run with optimum efficiency will be much larger and the credit facilities will have to be revived and extended as early as possible.

The job of planning in this sector is bound to be extremely difficult. The detailed physical requirements will have to be matched with financial flows and to avoid inefficiencies, the decision-making will have to be as decentralized as possible. The parameters of the Government action will have to be carefully chosen so that the private profit motives can be controlled and the behaviour of managers and workers properly regulated together with the efficient operation of production activities.

This is easier said than done. But still there is a genuine scope for hope, as this is the first popular government of liberated Bangla Desh which can demand and get sacrifice and dedicated effort from the people in the great task of economic reconstruction.

BOUDHAYAN CHATTOPADHYAY

RECONSTRUCTION OF BANGLA DESH—AND OF INDIA

Basic Premise

NO ECONOMY—NO matter how "mixed" it is—in so far as it is basically a market economy with the private sector predominant can escape projecting its own internal compulsions of capital accumulation on to its external economic relations. Consequently, it is unlikely that we shall succeed in suspending the operation of the internal modes of capital accumulation in the sphere of our economic relations with Bangla Desh, except in the very short run. If such modes of accumulation extent in our own economy militate against the objective of growth with equity for our own country, they will do all the more so vis-a-vis any other country. In the case of Bangla Desh, however, we cannot just allow this to happen in our own national interest. Consequences of a loss of goodwill in Bangla Desh will *not* remain confined within Bangla Desh. The backlash will engulf the whole of Eastern India.

Once the initial phase of political euphoria is over, economic calculations are bound to come into play. And, there is nothing intrinsically wrong about that either. Both trading and non-trading gains are likely to be quite high for both the countries, given the resource endowments of the two parts of the subcontinent. What matters, however, is: in whose interests are the economic calculations to be carried out?

This question becomes particularly relevant in view of the several outstanding features of our private sector characterizing the process of capital accumulation in the Indian economy to-day. Some of these are:

(a) In many of the major branches of our organized sector, foreign collaboration capital plays an important role;

(b) In our foreign trade, both the degree of monopoly and the extent of foreign control are higher than what they are in the domestic economy;

(c) Indian business, big and small, has pronounced preferences for quick profit-earning modes of operation, with strongly entrenched mercantilist motives.

Because of the projection of these built-in characteristics of our internal modes of capital accumulation, on to the sphere of our economic relations with the countries of the third world in Asia and Africa, India's image has often got tarnished in these countries.

We have, consequently, the following conundrum: India's economic relations in Bangla Desh cannot simply be built as an extension of the logic of our internal capital accumulation without jeopardizing the future political relations; on the other hand, these economic relations cannot also be built on political considerations only, in the long run, contrary to the dictates of the logic of our internal capital accumulation.

Some Possible Features of the Trade Relations

The dilemma is likely to be all the more acute in the case of Bangla Desh because of the following possible features of the trade relations between the two countries:

(*a*) It has been claimed sometimes that the economies of Bangla Desh and India (Eastern India in particular) are complementary. The fact that 80 per cent of pre-partition East Bengal's trade was with Eastern India is sometimes mentioned in this context. This is a totally false premise to build on. Pre-partition East Bengal was the agricultural hinterland of the Calcutta conurbation as an integral part of the colonial exigencies of the metropolitan power. Restoration of that "complementarity" would, in fact, reproduce in a worsened form the "complementarity" between the erstwhile eastern and western wings of Pakistan.

In fact, it may even be claimed that the dualistic colonial industrialization and commercialization of agriculture implicit in this so-called "complementarity", was one of the factors making for the partition of Bengal. One should, therefore, never even think in terms of this kind of "complementarity". Bangla Desh has become free not to become an agricultural appendage of the industries in Eastern India.

(*b*) Nevertheless, there is no escape from the eventuality that, for quite some years to come, the pattern of trade flows between Bangla Desh and India would consist of flows of primary produce from the former and of manufactures from the latter. The usual question of the probable worsening of the terms of trade of the primary produce exporter would crop up. In fact, Bangla Desh has started by devaluing her rupee to the level of parity with the Indian rupee, which implies a once-over deterioration in her terms of trade with India to start with, unless export duties are pushed up—a very unlikely eventuality.

As late as the middle of December 1971, 47 Pakistani rupees

were exchanging for 55 Indian rupees on the Hong Kong market. This option would no longer be available to Bangla Desh. The Bangla Desh currency would have to share all the vicissitudes of the Indian currency for quite some years to come. Indian policy makers should, therefore, take into account the effects on Bangla Desh's foreign exchange earnings and terms of trade when they indulge in their bouts of devaluation after every war with Pakistan. All the more so since Bangla Desh can hardly hope to gain anything from a currency depreciation because her two major exports, jute and tea, do not enjoy price-elasticities of world demand greater than unity.

(c) In the world market for Jute, Pakistan and India have traditionally constituted a situation of competitive duopoly, with Pakistan acting as the price-setter. Bangla Desh, which produced all of Pakistan's jute, enjoyed, and will continue to enjoy, what Adam Smith would call "absolute advantage" in the production of jute.

Acting as the price-setter, Pakistan was, till recently, under-quoting India by two to five per cent in hessian, and as much as 30 per cent in sacking. India's sacking exports declined from 3,12,000 tonnes in 1960 to 94,000 tonnes in 1968, while those of Pakistan increased from 1,24,000 tonnes to 2,43,000 tonnes over the same period. And, the western world market for jute is a shrinking market because of the challenge of the synthetics. Even in carpet backing, which was supposed to offset the shrinking demand for the traditional hessian and sacking, the share of jute in the United States carpet backings came down from 80.6 per cent in 1968 to 61.6 per cent in 1970, that of synthetics having gone up from 16 per cent to 33 per cent. Indian exports of jute manufactures rose by Rs 17.88

crores over April-July 1971, when Pakistan was virtually out of the market.

Nothing should be done to deprive Bangla Desh of the fruits of the absolute advantage that she enjoys in the production of raw jute and jute goods.

(d) Bangla Desh is not likely to be able to substantially reduce her deficit in rice in the near future. Between 1.7 and 2 million tonnes of rice will need to be imported. This is so particularly because the proportion of rice production entering the marketing channels is just about 10 per cent.

The question of the rice-deficit assumes particular importance in view of the fact that the high precipitation and the absence of water control systems in Bangla Desh would rule out the adoption of the HYV rice on a large scale in the main *aman* rice crop. In the near future, some advance could perhaps be registered in the *boro* crop, provided the large surface run-off can be impounded to raise the cropping intensity of rice lands. The adoption of HYV technology would also come up against the obstacle of extensive share cropping. Moreover, there have been reports of large scale destruction of the bullock population. One estimate puts the loss at 1.5 million.

While for some months to come India will have to meet the foodgrains deficit, having to rush possibly about 2 lakh tonnes every month, it is unlikely that the rice-deficit can be met by India over a longer period. The large rice-surpluses of Burma and Thailand need to be drawn upon.

These features taken together raise a number of issues of long-term policy which will be considered hereafter.

The Possibility of a Large Trade Deficit

There is, however, another possibility which needs to be considered before we go into some of the policy-issues. And, that is the likely emergence of a large trade deficit between India and Bangla Desh.

Tables 1 through 4 give a bird's eye view of Bangla Desh's trade and production structure.[1]

TABLE 1

FOREIGN TRADE OF BANGLA DESH

	International	With West Pakistan	Total (Rs Crores)
1960-61			
Exports	125.9	36.4	162.3
Imports	101.4	82.6	184.0
Balance	+ 24.5	— 46.2	— 21.7
1968-69			
Exports	154.3	87.1	241.4
Imports	185.0	138.5	323.5
Balance	— 30.7	— 51.4	— 82.1

Assuming that the total trade turnover of Bangla Desh would be around Rs 800 crores, taking into account the normal growth rates and changes in prices and exchange rates since 1968-69, and assuming further that the trade with India will substitute for not only the trade with West Pakistan but also for a major part of the international account, the trade turnover with India may be as much as Rs 600 crores, i.e., nearly

[1] The figures in these tables are in Pakistan currency at the prices and exchange rates prevailing then.

75 per cent of the total turnover, for some time to come.   In fact, in the initial stages the figure may be even higher.   For one thing, the costs of rehabilitation have sometimes been put at Rs 700 crores, of which not more than Rs 250 crores can be raised from inside Bangla Desh.

It is difficult to see how Bangla Desh can hope to export more than Rs 200 crores worth of goods and services to India, inclusive of the substantial transit income that is likely to arise out of the goods traffic along rail and water routes connecting Eastern India through Bangla Desh. That suggests a trade deficit of around Rs 200 crores, implying a corresponding magnitude of capital outflow from India into Bangla Desh.

TABLE 2

BANGLA DESH'S EXPORTS (FORMERLY SENT TO
WEST PAKISTAN)

Commodity	1968-69 (Rs crores)
Primary	
Betelnuts	0.85
Spices	0.98
Wood and timber	1.17
Others	7.85
Others	
Tea	22.89
Jute goods	14.22
Paper and paper board	9.10
Matches	3.17
Leather	2.96
All other Articles	16.27
Foreign merchandise	0.28
Total	87.12

It is this possibility which opens up the prospect of economic compulsions forcing the Governments of India and Bangla Desh to consider the movement of Indian big capital into Bangla Desh. "Indian" big capital would include, in this case, foreign capital located in India—particularly British capital. The UK could not have behaved in the UN the way she did, without expectation of some pay-off. West German and Japanese capital would step in as close seconds to the British.

Nobody should underestimate the overwhelming compulsions under which the economy and Government of Bangla Desh would have to seek capital resources. For one thing, Bangla Desh is one of the most densely populated areas of the world. Her population density is more than twice that of India, and is considerably higher than that of Ceylon. Potential capital resources have been drained out of Bangla Desh for more than two hundred years now. She has virtually no minerals. Her major export, staple, jute, faces a shrinking world market. She has only plentiful labour and water resources and considerable potential for fishery, forestry and paper pulp. Clearly, the strategy for her would be to build a fairly egalitarian economy based on intensive use of labour, water and land.

With a rather slow gradient, however, the development of the hydel power potential of the massive discharges carried by her rivers will require an integrated approach involving the whole of Eastern India so that the potential of the Brahmaputra and the North Bengal rivers can be tapped in an integrated manner all along the eastern states of India and Bangla Desh. A single electricity grid and a single water resources grid for the whole of eastern India and Bangla Desh seem to be very much on the agenda.

No private capitalist initiative can possibly conceive of facing up to this major challenge. On the other hand, there are certain built-in factors which may prompt big capital, Indian and foreign, located in India, to try to move into Bangla

TABLE 3

BANGLA DESH'S REQUIREMENTS (FORMERLY IMPORTED FROM WEST PAKISTAN)

Commodity	1968-69 (Rs crores)
Primary	
Oilseeds	11.50
Raw cotton	15.78
Tobacco	10.14
Foodgrains	14.92
All other commodities	10.38
Others	
Cotton fabrics	21.72
Cotton yarn and thread	6.12
Machinery	6.64
Drugs and medicines	5.39
Tobacco manufactures	2.22
Metal manufactures	1.88
Rape and mustard oil	0.75
Rubber goods	1.45
Paper and paper board	2.61
Vegetable oil non-essential	1.12
Cement	7.02
All other commodities	14.63
Foreign merchandise	4.29
Total	138.54

SOURCE: *The Economic Times.*

TABLE 4

IMPACT OF SEPARATE BANGLA DESH ON PAKISTAN'S
ECONOMY

Item	Pakistan	Bangla Desh	Percentage share of Bangla Desh to total (i.e. the loss to Pakistan)
1. Population (million)	126*	75*	59.5
2. Agriculture (1969-70) (000 tons)			
(a) Rice	14162	11816	83.4
(b) Food crops	23365	11998	51.4
(c) Seasamum	36	30	83.3
(d) Jute	1319	1319	100.0
(e) Tea	298	29.8	100.0
(f) Tobacco	161	41	25.5
(g) Sugarcane	33370	7418	22.2
3. Industry (1969-70)			
(a) Tea (lakh lbs)	696	696	100.0
(b) Cigarettes (crore nos)	4022	1778	44.2
(c) Cotton yarn (crore lbs)	70.8	10.6	15.0
(d) Jute goods (000 tons)	580	580	100.0
(e) Urea (000 tons)	297.4	94.3	31.7
(f) Safety matches (lakhgross boxes)	140.7	129.6	92.1
(g) Sulphuric acide (000 tons)	37.5	6.5	17.3
(h) Printing paper (000 tons)	21.4	21.4	100.0
(i) Writing paper (000 tons)	10.3	10.3	100.0
(j) Packing paper (000 tons)	10.5	10.5	100.0
(k) Newsprint (000 tons)	35.7	35.7	100.0
4. Exports (Rs crores)	333.71	167.01	50.0
5. Public finance (Rs crores) (1970-71 Budget)			
(a) Tax revenue from customs	181	98*	54.1
(b) Central excise	286	154*	53.8
(c) Income tax	118	64*	54.2
(d) Sales tax	78	42*	53.8
(e) Others	18	10*	55.6

*Estimated.
SOURCE: *The Economic Times*, 17 December 1971.

Desh in the form of joint ventures or otherwise. In jute, British-Indian capital located in India would have every reason to try to subordinate the jute interests in Bangla Desh— a large part of which would now be in the public sector—to their own requirements. In tea, with 60 per cent of Bangla Desh tea under British control, it should be so easy to produce collusive arrangements across the border, particularly because the trade channels and the auction proceedings are almost entirely in British hands.

A Jute Community and, Ceylon obliging, a Tea Community, would be very much on the agenda. But, by themselves, these commodity pool arrangements are not at all inconsistent with the consolidation of the overall domination of British-Indian big capital.

Operations of the MRTP Act and the Monopolies Commission provide another set of incentives for large houses located in India, Indian or foreign, to undertake expansion just across the border to evade the inquisition. If a Customs Union and a Payments Union also come into being, embracing Bangla Desh and India, all the scale economies would be available to such ventures of private capital, along with the benefits of a low-wage economy. This has to be viewed in the context of the new-found enthusiasm of Indian big capital to seek joint ventures with Western capital in the developing countries of Asia and Africa. An investment guarantee scheme to provide risk coverage to such Indian private ventures abroad at the cost of the public exchequer is also reportedly on the anvils of the relevant ministries of the Government of India. On the other hand, the existence of certain indigenous interests in Bangla Desh who may seek to prop themselves up with the help of Indian and British capital, cannot be ruled out either.

Some Policy Issues

1. *A Massive Hydel Power and Water Resource Development Programme.* The Government of Bangla Desh and the Awami League have been committed to nationalization of key industries and financial institutions. It is unlikely, however, that they will succeed in touching the business interests other than those of the West Pakistanis and the collaborators. They are also likely to be in a hurry to get access to international aid. If to this are added the compulsions of capital accumulation projected through the Indian private sector, it is quite on the cards that the prodigious labour resources of Bangla Desh would attract considerable private capital investments from India and elsewhere.

This will, however, have several consequences on Bangla Desh:

(a) It will distort both the distribution of income and the mix of the private and public sectors in Bangla Desh;

(b) It may perhaps perpetuate the balance-of-payments gap;

(c) It will divert resources from the more promising and effective lines of development based on intensive use of labour, land and water along egalitarian directions.

So far as India is concerned, the only way out seems to be to restrict the capital outflows to inter-governmental agencies only, and to institutionalize these in the form of a jointly administered development fund devoted to the integrated development of hydel power and water resource management over the whole of Eastern India and Bangla Desh. It is only through sharing of the non-trading gains that a trade-off can be found for the possible large trade deficit.

About a decade back, a study sponsered by the FAO had

spelt out a long-term perspective plan for the whole of the
Lower Ganges-Brahmaputra basin precisely on these terms.
India cannot effectively use the potential of the Brahmaputra
in Assam and of the North Bengal rivers without the free
involvement and agreement of Bangla Desh.   And, the massive
external economy effects of such a programme for both Eastern
India and Bangla Desh should more than pay off the foreseeable
commitments of Indian capital funds.   Of course, the programme would require institutionalized foreign assistance.
This is an eminently eligible field for the USSR to step in.

Such a programme would also permit a wide spectrum of
choices of technique so as to allow for massive applications of
human labour of which there is no shortage in the eastern
region of the subcontinent.

2.   *The Substance of Economic Integration.*   A Jute Community, a Tea Community (including Ceylon) and, hopefully,
a Rice Community (including Burma and Thailand), and
Customs and Payments Unions with Bangla Desh would
certainly constitute an eminently eligible package.   These
would also help project India's altered position in the power
balance in South and South-East Asia.   But, all such attempts
at regional and sub-regional integration in this part of the world
have so far foundered on the bedrock of suspicion that the
smaller countries have harboured about the intentions of Japan
at one end of the scale and of India at the other, because of the
altogether unequal levels of industrial development.   Com-
modity-wise sub-regional groupings such as the Coconut
Community, the Rubber Community, and the Jute, Tea or
Rice Communities have certainly a more promising future
than efforts at total regional integration.   Similarly, a Shipping
Pool could also play a very important role in breaking through

the barriers of the so-called Conferences.

A Jute Community of India and Bangla Desh, and, Ceylon obliging, a Tea Community could play a seminal role in initiating the movement for sub-regional and regional integration. The dollar crisis, the ensuing battle between Japan and the USA in the Far East in the seventies, and the impending threat of the Japanese Latin Americanization of South and South-East Asia[2] have together created a situation favourable for an integration movement in South and South-East Asia.

But, once again, India can play a leading role in initiating this movement starting with the Jute Community *only* if she can disabuse her policy-makers of the idea that India's interests also lie in somehow acquiring a share of the market in this area along with the USA and Japan—even if she has to do so as a poor relation. It is only by projecting a consistent anti-imperialist stance wedded to the objective of self-reliant growth that she can hope to make good the lost ground. And, Bangla Desh is the test case.

Neither by promoting investment guarantee schemes for export of Indian private capital abroad—an altogether futile aping of American, West German or Japanese behaviour—nor by helping Indian private capital to embark on "joint ventures" as junior partners of West German or US or Japanese capital in the developing countries of Asia and Africa, can the battle be won. Surely, there must be better ways of wiping out excess capacities in Indian industries. Such policies would only succeed in drawing upon us, also, the wrath of resurgent nationalism in this part of the world.

India can project such an image and pass the test of Bangla

[2] See author's "The Japanese Scene" in *Indian Left Review*, Vol. I., No. 7.

Desh *only* if she chooses, as rapidly as she can, to alter the premises of capital accumulation in her own economy. Faced with sagging domestic saving and investment rates, a drastic change in the premises of our own accumulation is also the only way out of our own crisis.

Throwing off the yoke of foreign capital, the dependence on foreign aid and on the vagaries of the western capitalist world market, constitutes the first step in this direction. To start with, nationalization of jute and tea, and formulation of a well thought out pricing-and-market sharing agreement with Bangla Desh that allows her to enjoy the fruits of her natural advantages, backed up by a joint crash programme of the development of indigenous R and D for the diversification of jute manufactures, could constitute the substance of the first steps of the movement for economic integration in the region. At the same time, the whole question of Indian private capital outflows—joint ventures or otherwise—should be brought within the purview of the Monopolies Commission and the MRTP Act.

It needs to be reiterated again that it is not so much the *form* of economic integration, but its substance, the underlying premises of capital accumulation, that matters.

3. *The Question of Relative Prices.* The Indian industrial structure is a high cost structure, thanks to excess capacities and inefficient and protectionist practices. The fact that Bangla Desh would be exporting mostly primary produce to India and would be importing manufactures from India, raises in an essential way the question of relative prices and the terms of trade. It has to be borne in mind that precisely such a pattern of trade led to unfavourable terms of trade for the peasant of what was once East Pakistan and thereby served as an ins-

trument of resource transfer from the eastern to the western wing. This is the most important single reason why not only should private trade be ruthlessly controlled, but even inter-governmental transactions should strictly adhere to international prices. Even then the terms of trade may not be favourable to Bangla Desh. But, at least, India's hands would be clean.

There is some evidence to suggest that our trade links with the socialist countires have tended to stabilize the prices of our primary exports. Possibilities of extending corresponding terms to Bangla Desh should also be explored.

4. *Model Villages of Cooperative Self-Management.* It is clear that a nation of 30 million refugees and homeless can be rehabilitated only by harnessing the energy of the masses themselves. The 200,000 young fighters of all kinds, sections of whom are now being converted into the national people's militia in Bangla Desh, can serve as the driving force of a mass rehabilitation programme at the village level. There has been some talk in certain influential Bangla Desh circles that given a suitable policy of land reform (with a ceiling in the range of 30 to 50 bighas, 2 million acres of surplus land may become available), consolidation of holdings, pooled supply of inputs, including power tillers to substitute for the lost 1.5 million cattle, the fact of national disaster can be turned into a national blessing and a Kibutz type movement of model villages of cooperative self-management can be brought into being. Given a certain supply of brickmaking non-coking coal, pro-vision can be made for the Bengal peasant to build for his family *pucca* dwellings for the first time in history.

No efforts should be spared on our part to enable the people of Bangla Desh to help themselves. Maybe, what they shall be doing tomorrow, we will start doing the day after. Let their reconstruction be ours also, just as the threat to their existance became a threat to our existence.

Only by moving step by step along these directions can we get away from the conundrum staring us in the face. That will also necessarily involve us in the process of altering the premises of capital accumulation extant in our own "mixed" market economy.

APPENDICES

OPENING SPEECH BY DR V. K. R. V. RAO AT THE PANEL DISCUSSION ON BANGLA DESH

We have arranged this panel discussion on the Economic Prospects of Bangla Desh under the joint auspices of the Institute of Economic Growth and the India International Centre. This is a first preliminary discussion and we hope that later on opportunity will be forthcoming for more detailed discussion and analysis of different aspects of Bangla Desh economy and more especially ways and means by which mutual cooperation between the Governments and peoples of India and Bangla Desh can help in promoting the welfare and prosperity of the people of Bangla Desh.

The immediate problem confronting Bangla Desh is one of the restoration of her economy and the rehabilitation and reconstruction of its country following the damage that war and oppression of West Pakistani rulers have brought to the country and the people of Bangla Desh. While the problem is immense, it is also important to emphasize that Bangla Desh faces these problems, not only of rehabilitation but also of reconstruction and economic development, from a much better position of strength and confidence, now that it is an independent country and not a colonial area of West Pakistan.

In my opinion, there are three major factors which give a room for optimism regarding the economic prospects of Bangla Desh and its ability to utilize fully and fruitfully its immense natural resources for the benefit of its masses. These are:

(*a*) Removal of the dead weight of colonial and metropolitan rule imposed by the rulers of West Pakistan. Thus, during the period when what is now Bangla Desh formed a part of Pakistan and was called East Pakistan, the disparity between East Pakistan and West Pakistan grew apace and became substantial in magnitude. Thus, the annual disparity in electricity production in terms of kwh per capita increased from 7.4 in the pre-plan period to 54.4 during the Third Plan period of Pakistan. During the same period, the annual disparity in per capita private investment between the two parts increased from Rs 6.6 to Rs 41.9; and in per capita imports from Rs 18 to Rs 37.1. The result of all this was that the per capita income of what is now Bangla Desh was not only very much below the per capita income of West Pakistan but also that the annual disparity between the two per capita figures increased from Rs 46 to Rs 102. All this will now go, as Bangla Desh is a free country and it will have a government which is committed to the welfare of its people. The fresh air of freedom that has now come to Bangla Desh will enable that country to go ahead purposefully with building up the infra-structure and investment that are needed to place Bangla Desh on the firm road of a high rate of economic growth.

(b) The economic consequences of the partition of the two countries in 1947 may not have had such adverse consequences on what is now Bangla Desh but for the anti-Indian posture and hate-India mania which seized the rulers of Pakistan. As a result of this policy on their part and their control over what is now Bangla Desh, they brought about most uneconomic diversion of trade, commerce, employment and investment from their normal channels the main victim of which policy was Bangla Desh. Thus, Bangla Desh had to go a long distance to get coal that it would have got easily from nearby India. Similarly, with a huge market in India for their fish, they had to seek markets in distant places. Also when opportunities for the acquisition of technical skills and know-how were available nearby, the sons and daughters of Bangla Desh had to go long distances for acquiring these skills and even such opportunities as were given to them were inadequate as compared to what were given to the sons and daughters of West Pakistan. The eastern part of the subcontinent, of which India is one member, has an identity of economic interest and a mutual rewarding complimentarity that was broken not by the political separation of East Bengal but by the anti-Indian policies that were forced on East Bengal by the Pakistan rulers. This handicap will now disappear with the emergence of an Independent Bangla Desh and with the warm feelings of friendship and goodwill that Independent Bangla Desh will have for India. This friendship and goodwill will make it possible for a new era of economic cooperation between Bangla Desh and the Indian wing of the eastern part of the subcontinent. And this will result in mutual benefit and especially to the benefit of the people of Bangla Desh.

(c) The removal of these twin handicaps on the economic growth of what is now Bangla Desh, namely, the handicaps of West Pakistan imperialism and the unnatural diversion of economic transactions resulting from West Pakistani hatred for India, the removal of these handicaps will immensely strengthen the economic prospects of Bangla Desh. Even more than this is the great strength that will now emerge from the national will of Bangla Desh that has shown itself in the way it has won freedom from its oppressors. With the handicaps resulting from association with Pakistan now removed, and with the national will that has now emerged, the economic prospects of Bangla Desh are very bright indeed;

and I have no doubt that, in due course, that country will have a rate of economic growth that will compare well with the most advanced among the developing economies.

In this great task of reconstruction and development of Bangla Desh, India's cooperation is freely available and to the extent it is desired by Bangla Desh. I have no doubt that at the governmental level this cooperation will take many fruitful and mutually rewarding forms. I shall, however, not dilate on this as I have no authority to speak on behalf of the Indian Government. I would like, however, to make three suggestions which involve the cooperation and participation of the Indian people in the great efforts that the people of Bangla Desh will be putting in for their rehabilitation and development. These suggestions are:

(*i*) The Indian Government can give an opportunity to the Indian people to show their friendship for the people of Bangla Desh by being given the opportunity to subscribe to a special Bangla Desh reconstruction loan which could be floated by the Indian Government. The proceeds of this loan could be made over as a loan to the Government of Bangla Desh but without any interest charges for the first five years, period of repayment to be from 25 to 30 years after the termination of this five-year period, and the rate of interest charged during that period being lower than the rate of interest that would be charged by the World Bank on its loans to India. Such a loan will be consistent with self respect and at the same time will give an opportunity to the people of this country, irrespective of their economic status, to show concretely their friendship for and interest in the welfare of the people of Bangla Desh.

(*ii*) A Bangla Desh Development Corps could be formed in India consisting of young volunteers with different types of technical, scientific and development skills, whose services could be used by the Government and people of Bangla Desh on the same lines as the services of several volunteer corps formed by the international youth associations have been used in the past by some developing countries. These Indian youngsters will work shoulder to shoulder with the youngsters of Bangla Desh with true dedication and for the rehabilitation of Bangla Desh and will take for themselves a remuneration which would cover only their living expenses. I would further suggest that to facilitate the recruitment of such volunteers, the Government of India should guarantee the members of this corps employment when they return to India at the end of three years, which is the period for which they should be prepared to serve in Bangla Desh. Our Government should also, when giving them employment on their return to India, take into account the three years' service they have put in in Bangla Desh for determining their remuneration and seniority in service. This will give an excellent opportunity for the youth of India to work in co-operation and partnership with the youth of Bangla Desh in the glorious task of national reconstruction.

(*iii*) Close cooperation can be established on a non-official basis between the intellectuals, scientists and other professionals of India with their counterparts in Bangla Desh in such a manner as to enable them to use their joint skills for the welfare and prosperity of the masses of Bangla Desh. As one example as to what can be done—I am referring to something which comes within the field of my own intellectual discipline—I hope it will be possible to arrange a seminar of Indian and Bangla Desh economists and developmental social scientists some time in October next year, but not in Delhi, in Dacca. I hope at such a seminar we could put our heads together and analyse and discuss the different problems of the Bangla Desh economy and also try to suggest measures for their solution, including the role that mutual cooperation between the two countries can play in this matter.

TABLE I

COMPARATIVE LEVELS OF DEVELOPMENT: BANGLA DESH
AND WEST PAKISTAN

Variable	Units of Measurement	Year	Bangla Desh	West Pakistan
1. Population	Million	1949-50	43.0	35.8
		1969-70	70.2	57.2
2. Area	Sq. miles	1961	55,126	310,403
3. Density	Persons per sq. mile	1961	922	138
4. Gross national product	Rupees million	1949-50	12,360	12,106
		1969-70	23,783	28,596
5. Per capita income	Rupees	1949-50	287	338
		1969-70	339	500
6. Gross investment ratio	Percentage	1950-55	5.0	12.3
		1963-68	13.3	20.8
7. Gross manufactured product	Rupees million	1949-50	472	961
		1964-65	1536	2904
8. Share of manufactured product in GNP	Percentage	1949-50	3.80	7.94
		1964-65	7.12	15.15
9. Production of principal foodcrops	000 tons	1955-60 (average)	7,590	6,301
		1969-70	11,998	11,367
10. Exports	Rupees million	1949-50	628.8	565.1
		1969-70	1670.1	1667.0
11. Interwing exports	Rupees million	1949-50	32.3	229.2
		1969-70	916.1	1652.2
12. Railway net freight	Tons million	1949-50	655	1807
		1968-69	725	4761
13. Road mileage	Miles	1954-55	320	7980
		1968-69	2388	10,609
14. Electricity	Million kwh	1949-50	13.6	150.8
		1969-70	1300.0	6700.0
15. Literacy	Percentage	1961	21.5	16.3

SOURCES: (1) *Five Year Plans*, Pakistan; (2) *Pakistan Economic Survey*, 1970-71; (3) *Census of Pakistan*, 1961.

TABLE 2

TABLE 2

POPULATION CHARACTERISTICS: BANGLA DESH, 1961

Characteristics	Persons (000)	Males (000)	Females (000)
1. Population	50,840	26,349	24,491
(i) Urban	2,641	1,551	1,090
As % of 1	5.2	5.9	4.5
(ii) Rural	48,199	24,798	23,401
As % 1	94.8	94.1	95.5
2. Civilian labour force	17,443	14,802	2,641
As % of 1	34.3	56.2	10.7
(i) Agriculturists	14,872	12,452	2,420
As % of 2	85.3	84.1	91.6
(ii) Non-agriculturists	2,571	2,350	221
As % of 2	14.7	15.9	8.4
3. Literates	8,955	6,846	2,109
As % of 1 (5 years & above)	21.5	31.5	10.7
With formal education	7,505	5,761	1,774
As % of 1 (5 years & above)	18.0	26.4	8.8

SOURCE: *Census of Pakistan, 1961.*

TABLE 3

POPULATION BY EDUCATIONAL LEVELS: BANGLA DESH, 1961

Educational Level	Persons (000)	Males (000)	Females (000)
1. Literates with formal education	7,505 (100.0)	5,761 (100.0)	1,744 (100.0)
2. Primary school	5,688 (75.8)	4,117 (71.5)	1,571 (90.1)
3. Middle secondary school	1,480 (19.7)	1,324 (23.0)	156 (8.9)
4. Matriculation	247 (3.3)	235 (4.1)	12 (0.7)
5. Intermediate	53 (0.7)	50 (0.8)	3 (0.2)
6. Degree	28 (0.4)	27 (0.5)	1 (0.05)
7. Higher degree	7 (0.09)	6.8 (0.1)	0.3 (0.02)
8. Oriental	2 (0.02)	1.6 (0.03)	0.2 (0.01)

NOTE : Figures in brackets are percentage of Literates with formal education.

SOURCE : Same as Table 2.

TABLE 4

PRINCIPAL CROPS: BANGLA DESH, 1969-70

Crop	Area (000 acres)	Production (000 tons)	Yields (mds)
1. Rice	25,486	11,816	12.6
2. Wheat	296	103	9.5
3. Maize	8	3	10.2
4. Barley	73	19	7.1
5. Gram	173	57	9.0
6. Sugarcane	399	7418	506.7
7. Rape and mustard	536	126	6.3
8. Seasum	125	30	6.6
9. Jute	2465	1319	14.1
10. Cotton	34	2	1.9
11. Tea	107	29.8	7.6
12. Tobacco	113	41	9.5

SOURCE : *Pakistan Economic Survey*, 1970-71.

TABLE 5

SELECTED MANUFACTURING INDUSTRIES: BANGLA DESH
1969-70

Industries	Unit of measurement of production	Production	Number of mills (Jan. 1969)
1. Food manufacturing :			
(i) Tea	Lakh lbs	696	117
(ii) Sugar	000 tons	89	10
(iii) Hydrogenated veg. oils	000 tons	6.4	19
2. Tobacco manufacturing: Cigarettes	Crores nos	1778	15
3. Textiles manufacturing:			
(i) Cotton yarn	Crore lbs	10.6	46
(ii) Cotton cloth	Crore yds	5.9	
(iii) Art silk & rayon cloth	Lakh yds	49.7	11
4. Jute goods	000 tons	580	41
5. Rubber manufacturing: Tyers & Tubes	Lakh Nos	2.8	2
6. Chemical fertilizer & chemical manufacturing:			
(i) Urea	000 tons	94.3	1
(ii) Sulphuric acid	000 tons	6.5	1
(iii) Safety matches	40-60-sticks lakh gross boxes	129.6	20
7. Cement	Lakh tons	0.53	1
8. Paper manufacturing:			2
(i) Printing paper	000 tons	21.4	
(ii) Writing paper	000 tons	10.3	
(iii) Packing and other paper	000 tons	10.5	
(iv) Newsprint	000 tons	35.7	
9. Paints and varnishes	000 cwt	4.7	10

SOURCES: (1) *Pakistan Economic Survey.* 1970-71;
(2) *Monthly Statistical Bulletin*, Pakistan, March 1969.

TABLE 6

EXPORTS OF PRINCIPAL COMMODITIES: BANGLA DESH
1967-68

Commodity	Unit of measure- ment of quantity	Quantity	Value (Rs 000)
1. Raw jute	Tons	666,788	758,898
2. Raw cotton	Tons	722	1,541
3. Raw hides skins	Cwt	2,839	2,031
4. Cotton twist yarn & thread	ooo lbs	2,884	4,991
5. Cotton fabrics	ooo yds	6,308	6,307
6. Fish	Cwt	34,726	11,841
7. Jute manufacturers			
(i) Jute bags	Tons	227,252	273,641
(ii) Jute fabrics	Tons	204,872	319,099
(iii) Jute carpets	ooo sq.ft.	900	2,560
(iv) Rope & twine of jute		—	6446
(v) Jute yarn	ooo lbs	4,672	3,764
8. Cottonwaste	Cwt	6,618	320
9. Leather	Cwt	101,695	43,057

SOURCES : *Monthly Statistical Bulletin*, Pakistan, September 1968.

TABLE 7

DISTRICT-WISE POPULATION, AREA & DENSITY: BANGLA DESH
1961

Districts	Population (000)	Area sq. miles	Density persons per sq. mile
1. Dacca	5,096	2,670	1,909
2. Mymensingh	7,019	6,151	1,141
3. Faridpur	3,179	2,424	1,311
4. Chittagong	2,983	2,619	1,131
5. Chittagong hill tracts	385	5,085	75
6. Noakhali	2,383	1,623	1,468
7. Comilla	4,389	2,446	1,794
8. Sylhet	3,490	4,736	737
9. Rajshahi	2,811	3,569	788
10. Dinajpur	1,710	2,593	659
11. Rangpur	3,796	3,358	1,130
12. Bogra	1,574	1,464	1,075
13. Pabna	1,959	1,693	1,157
14. Khulna	2,499	4,080	600
15. Bakerganj	4,261	3,590	1,187
16. Kushtia	1,166	1,323	882
17. Jessore	2,190	2,497	877

SOURCE: Statistical Digest of East Pakistan, 1966.

TABLE 8

DISTRICT-WISE URBAN AND RURAL POPULATION
BANGLA DESH, 1961

District	Population (000)	Urban (000)	Rural (000)
1. Dacca	5,096	754 (14.8)	4,342 (85.2)
2. Mymansingh	7,019	240 (3.4)	6,778 (96.6)
3. Faridpur	3,179	79 (2.5)	3,100 (97.5)
4. Chittagong	2,983	373 (12.5)	2,610 (87.5)
5. Chittagong hill tracts	385	23 (5.9)	362 (94.1)
6. Noakhali	2,383	34 (1.4)	2,349 (98.6)
7. Comilla	4,389	139 (3.2)	4,250 (96.8)
8. Sylhet	3,490	71 (2.0)	3,419 (98.0)
9. Rajshahi	2,811	120 (4.3)	2,691 (95.7)
10. Dinajpur	1,710	72 (4.2)	1,639 (95.8)
11. Rangpur	3,796	159 (4.2)	3,637 (95.8)
12. Bogra	1,574	47 (3.0)	1,527 (97.0)
13. Pabna	1,959	100 (5.1)	1,860 (94.9)
14. Khulna	2,449	173 (7.1)	2,276 (92.9)
15. Bakerganj	4,261	119 (2.8)	4,142 (97.2)
16. Kushtia	1,166	63 (5.4)	1,103 (94.6)
17. Jessore	2,190	75 (3.4)	2,115 (96.6)

NOTE: Figures in brackets are percentage of population.
SOURCE: Same as in Table 7.

TABLE 9

REGIONAL DISTRIBUTION OF GROSS NATIONAL PRODUCT—PAKISTAN
(Annual Averages)

Period	East Pakistan		West Pakistan		Pakistan		Disparity	
	Total (Rs crores)	Per capita (Rs)	Total (Rs crores)	Per capita (Rs)	Total (Rs crores)	Per capita (Rs)	Per capita (Rs)	Index (%)
Pre-Plan period	1352.4	297.6	1305.1	343.6	2657.5	318.6	46.0	100.0
First-Plan period	1414.0	275.7	1561.3	363.9	2975.3	315.9	88.2	191.7
Second-Plan period	1753.3	301.5	1912.3	393.2	3665.6	343.3	91.7	199.3
Third-Plan period	2131.1	330.7	2333.1	432.9	4464.2	377.3	102.2	222.2

SOURCES:
(i) 1949-50 to 1963-64: Khan, T. M. and Bergan, A., *Measurement of Structural Change in Pakistan Economy: A Review of National Income Estimates*; 1949/50-1963/64: *Pakistan Development Review*, Summer, 1966.

(ii) 1964-65: *Third Five Year Plan*, Government of Pakistan.

(iii) 1965-66 to 1967-68: Based on growth rate given in *Economy of Pakistan*, 1948-68, Government of Pakistan, Economic Adviser, Ministry of Finance.(Third Plan Period covers up to 1967-68 only.)

TABLE 10

SHARE OF INDUSTRIAL SECTORS IN GROSS PROVINCIAL PRODUCT—PAKISTAN

Annual Averages

Period	East Pakistan			West Pakistan			Pakistan		
	Industrial* %	Mfg %	Large scale Mfg %	Industrial* %	Mfg %	Large scale Mfg %	Industrial* %	Mfg %	Large scale Mfg %
Pre-Plan period	4.9	4.2	1.0	12.0	9.5	4.1	8.4	6.8	2.5
First-Plan period	6.9	5.7	2.3	14.9	12.1	6.8	11.1	9.0	4.7
Second-Plan period	9.9	7.1	4.0	17.5	13.2	8.3	13.9	10.3	6.2
Thrid-Plan period	—	—	—	—	—	—	—	—	—

*Comprising mining, manufacturing, and construction.

TABLE 10 (continued)

SHARE OF INDUSTRIAL SECTORS IN GROSS PROVINCIAL PRODUCT—PAKISTAN

Annual Averages

| | Disparity | | | | | |
| | Differences | | | Index | | |
Period	Industrial (%)	Manufacturing (%)	Large scale mfg (%)	Industrial %	Manufacturing (%)	Large scale mfg (%)
Pre-Plan period	7.1	5.3	3.1	100.0	100.0	100.0
First-Plan period	8.0	6.4	4.5	112.7	120.7	145.1
Second-Plan period	7.6	6.1	4.3	107.0	115.1	138.7
Third-Plan period	—	—	—	—	—	—

SOURCE: Same as Table 9.

TABLE II

REGIONAL DISTRIBUTION OF PLAN DEVELOPMENT EXPENDITURE—PAKISTAN

Annual Averages

Plan period	East Pakistan		West Pakistan		Pakistan		Disparity	
	Total (Rs million)	Per capita (Rs)	Total (Rs million)	Per capita (Rs)	Total (Rs million)	Per capita (Rs)	Per capita (Rs)	Index (Percentage)
Pre-Plan period	378.0	8.3	818.0	21.5	1196.0	14.3	13.2	100.0
First-Plan period	678.0	13.2	1592.0	37.1	2270.0	24.1	23.9	181.1
Second-Plan period	1844.6	31.7	4212.6*	86.6	6108.3	57.2	54.9	415.9
Third-Plan period	2941.9	45.6	5817.2*	107.9	8159.1	74.0	62.3	471.9

SOURCES: (i) For Pre-Plan period (1950-55) and First Plan period (1955-60): Maqbul Haq, *The Strategy of Economic Planning; A Case Study of Pakistan.*

          (ii) For Second Plan period (1960-65): *Review of Second Five Year Plan,* Planning Commission, Pakistan.

          (iii) For Third Five-Year Plan period (1965/66 to 1967/68 only): *Mid-Term Review of Third Plan,* Planning Commission, Pakistan.

*Includes Indus Basin development expenditure.

TABLE 12

REGIONAL DISTRIBUTION OF PUBLIC SECTOR DEVELOPMENTAL EXPENDITURE : PAKISTAN
(PROVINCIAL PLUS CENTRAL)

Annual Averages

| Plan period | East Pakistan | | West Pakistan | | Pakistan | | Disparity | |
	Total (Rs million)	Per capita (Rs)	Total (Rs million)	Per capita (Rs)	Total (Rs million)	Per capita (Rs)	Percentage (Rs)	Index Percentage
Pre-Plan period	188.0	4.1	410.0	10.8	598.0	7.2	6.7	100.0
First-Plan period	394.0	7.7	926.0	21.6	1320.0	14.0	13.9	207.5
Second-Plan period	1231.8	21.1	2089.4	43.0	2790.0	26.1	21.9	326.8
Third-Plan period	2123.5	32.9	2885.8	53.5	5009.3	42.3	20.6	307.5

SOURCE: Same as in Table 11.

TABLE 13

REGIONAL DISTRIBUTION OF PROVINCIAL EXPENDITURE : PAKISTAN

Annual Averages

| Plan period | East Pakistan | | West Pakistan | | Pakistan | | Disparity | |
	Total (Rs million)	Per capita (Rs)	Total (Rs. million)	Per capita (Rs)	Total (Rs million)	Per capita (Rs)	Per capita (Rs)	Index (percentage)
Pre-Plan period	98.0	2.2	256.0	6.7	354.0	4.2	4.5	100.0
First-Plan period	216.0	4.2	418.0	9.7	634.0	6.7	5.5	122.2
Second-Plan period	1003.4	17.2	1138.4	23.4	2141.8	20.1	6.2	137.7
Third-Plan period	1788.5	27.8	1522.3	28.2	3310.8	27.9	0.4	8.8

SOURCE: Same as in Table 11.

TABLE 14

REGIONAL DISTRIBUTION OF CENTRAL EXPENDITURE: PAKISTAN

Annual Average

Plan period	East Pakistan		West Pakistan		Pakistan		Disparity	
	Total (Rs million)	Per capita (Rs)	Total (Rs million)	Per capita (Rs)	Total (Rs million)	Per capita (Rs)	Per capita (Rs)	Index (percentage)
Pre-Plan period	90.0	1.9	154.0	4.0	244.0	2.9	2.2	100.0
First-Plan period	178.0	3.5	508.0	11.8	686.0	7.3	8.3	377.3
Second-Plan period	228.4	3.9	951.0	19.6	1179.4	11.0	15.7	713.6
Third-Plan period	316.1	4.9	1337.5	24.8	1653.6	14.0	19.9	904.5

SOURCE: Same as in Table 11.

TABLE 15

REGIONAL DISTRIBUTION OF CENTRAL DEVELOPMENTAL ASSISTANCE : PAKISTAN

Annual Average

Plan periods	East Pakistan		West Pakistan		Pakistan		Disparity	
	Total (Rs. million)	Per capita (Rs.)	Total (Rs. million)	Per capita (Rs.)	Total (Rs. million)	Per capita (Rs.)	Per capita (Rs.)	Index (percentage)
Pre-Plan period	58.3	1.2	114.9	3.0	173.2	2.0	1.8	100.0
First-Plan period	272.7	5.3	401.7	9.3	674.4	7.1	4.0	222.2
Second-Plan period	887.7	15.2	874.4	17.9	1762.1	16.5	2.7	150.0
Third-Plan period*	1381.7	21.4	884.9	16.4	2266.6	19.1	—5.0	...

SOURCE: *The Budget in Brief*, 1969–70, Government of Pakistan, Ministry of Finance.
*Up to 1967–68 only.

TABLE 16

REGIONAL DISTRIBUTION OF LOANS SANCTIONED BY CENTRAL GOVERNMENT-SPONSORED FINANCIAL INSTITUTIONS: PAKISTAN

Annual Average

Plan period	East Pakistan		West Pakistan		Pakistan		Disparity	
	Total (Rs. million)	Per capita (Rs.)	Total (Rs. million)	Per capita (Rs.)	Total (Rs. million)	Per capita (Rs.)	Per capita (Rs.)	Index (percentage)
Pre-Plan period ⎱ First-Plan period ⎰	31.9	0.7	64.2	1.6	96.1	1.1	0.9	100.0
Second-Plan period	190.3	3.2	274.3	5.6	465.1	4.3	2.4	266.7
Third-Plan period	245.6	3.6	375.8	6.8	621.4	5.1	3.2	355.5

SOURCE: *Pakistan Economic Survey*, 1969-70, Economic Adviser to the Government of Pakistan, Ministry of Finance.
NOTE: Financial Corporations Comprising P.I.C.I.C., I.D.B.P., and A.D.B.P. only.

TABLE 17

REGIONAL DISTRIBUTION OF EXPENDITURE ON PHYSICAL INFRASTRUCTURE IN PUBLIC SECTOR: PAKISTAN*

Annual Average

Plan period	East Pakistan		West Pakistan		Pakistan		Disparity	
	Total (Rs. million)	Per capita (Rs.)	Total (Rs. million)	Per capita (Rs.)	Total (Rs. million)	Per capita (Rs.)	Per capita (Rs.)	Index (percentage)
First-Plan period	128.8	2.5	375.2	8.7	504.0	5.4	6.2	100.0
Second-Plan period	586.4	10.0	1477.9	30.4	2064.3	19.3	20.4	329.0
Third-Plan period	991.0	15.3	2138.0	39.7	3129.0	26.5	24.4	393.5

SOURCE: For First-Plan period: "The Role of the Public Sector in Economic Development in Pakistan" by M.A. Rahman, a paper contributed to the "Conference on Economic Development on South Asia, Ceylon; For the Second-Plan and the Third-Plan periods: Same as in Table 11.
* Expenditure on Water, Power and Transportation.

TABLE 18

REGIONAL DISTRIBUTION OF POWER PRODUCTION: PAKISTAN

Annual Average

Period	East Pakistan		West Pakistan		Pakistan		Disparity	
	Total (000Kwh)	Per capita (Kwh)	Total (000Kwh)	Per capita (Kwh)	Total (000Kwh)	Per capita (Kwh)	Per capita (Kwh)	Index (Percentage)
Pre-Plan period	22,125	0.49	299,519	7.89	321,644	3.86	7.40	100.0
First-Plan period	118,044	2.30	868,169	20.24	986,214	10.47	17.94	242.4
Second-Plan period	346,325	5.95	2,032,002	41.78	2,378,327	20.09	35.83	484.1
Third-Plan period	688,478	10.68	3,596,855	65.05	4,285,333	35.30	54.37	734.7

SOURCES: (1) *Monthly Statistical Bulletin*, December 1965, Government of Pakistan, C.S.O.;

(2) *Statistical Digest*, Government of East Pakistan, 1966;

(3) *Statistical Yearbook*, U.N., 1969.

TABLE 19

REGIONAL DISTRIBUTION OF NET FREIGHT TON MILES: PAKISTAN

Annual Average

Period	East Pakistan		West Pakistan		Pakistan		Disparity	
	Total (million ton miles)	Per capita (ton miles)	Total (million ton miles)	Per capita (ton miles)	Total (million ton miles)	Per capita (ton miles)	Per capita (ton miles)	Index (percentage)
Pre-Plan period	510.6	11.2	2703.4	71.2	3214.0	38.50	60.0	100.0
First-Plan period	755.8	14.7	3405.0	79.4	4160.8	44.20	64.7	107.8
Second-Plan period	985.6	16.9	4412.4	90.7	5398.0	50.54	73.8	114.0
Third-Plan period	815.4	12.6	4958.6	92.0	5774.0	48.79	79.4	132.3

SOURCE: Same as in Table 16.

TABLE 20

REGIONAL DISTRIBUTION OF PRIVATE SECTOR INVESTMENT: PAKISTAN

Annual Average

Plan period	East Pakistan		West Pakistan		Pakistan		Disparity	
	Total (Rs. million)	Per capita (Rs.)	Total (Rs. million)	Per capita (Rs.)	Total (Rs. million)	Per capita (Rs.)	Per capita (Rs.)	Index (percentage)
Pre-Plan period	190.0	4.1	408.0	10.7	598.0	7.2	6.6	100.0
First-Plan period	284.0	5.5	666.0	15.5	950.0	10.1	10.0	151.5
Second-Plan period*	612.8	10.5	2123.2	43.6	2736.0	25.6	33.1	501.5
Third-Plan period	837.5	13.0	2957.4	54.9	3794.9	32.1	41.9	634.8

*Regional distribution is based on the assumption that East Pakistan's share was 22.4 per cent (actual share for two last years of Second Plan).

SOURCE: Same as in Table 11.

TABLE 21

REGIONAL DISTRIBUTION OF FOREIGN EXCHANGE ASSISTANCE IN GOVERNMENT SECTOR: PAKISTAN

Annual Average

| Period | East Pakistan | | West Pakistan | | Pakistan | | Disparity | |
	Total (Rs. million)	Per capita (Rs.)	Total (Rs. million)	Per capita (Rs.)	Total (Rs. million)	Per capita (Rs.)	Per capita (Rs.)	Index
Pre-Plan period	3.2*	0.07	3.6**	0.09	6.8	0.08	0.02	100.0
First Plan period	42.7	0.83	60.0	1.39	102.7	1.09	0.56	217.8
Second Plan period	122.1	2.09	160.9	3.31	283.0	2.65	1.22	207.1
Third Plan period	289.2	4.49	304.4	5.65	593.6	5.02	1.16	207.1

SOURCE: Same as in Table 15.

*1954-55; **1952-53 to 1954-55.

TABLE 22

REGIONAL DISTRIBUTION OF IMPORTS: PAKISTAN

Annual Average

Plan period	East Pakistan		West Pakistan		Pakistan		Disparity	
	Total (Rs. million)	Per capita (Rs.)	Total (Rs. million)	Per capita (Rs.)	Total (Rs. million)	Per capita (Rs.)	Per capita (Rs.)	Index (percentage)
Pre-Plan period	439.3	9.7	1053.1	27.7	1492.4	17.9	18.0	100.0
First-Plan period	624.8	12.2	1325.0	30.9	1949.8	20.7	18.7	103.9
Second-Plan period	1211.2	20.8	2772.7	57.1	3983.9	37.3	36.3	201.7
Third-Plan period	1393.3	21.6	3244.9	58.7	4638.2	39.2	37.1	206.1

SOURCE: *Monthly Statistical Bulletin*, Jan. 1960 and March 1969, Government of Pakistan, C.S.O.

TABLE 23

REGIONAL DISTRIBUTION OF IMPORTS OF CAPITAL GOODS AND MATERIALS FOR CAPITAL GOODS: PAKISTAN

Annual Average

Plan period	East Pakistan		West Pakistan		Pakistan		Disparity	
	Total (Rs. millions)	Per capita (Rs.)	Total (Rs. millions)	Per capita (Rs.)	Total (Rs. millions)	Per capita (Rs.)	Per capita (Rs.)	Per capita Index (percentage)
Pre-Plan period	166.2	3.7	367.6	9.7	533.8	6.4	6.0	100.0
First-Plan period	268.4	5.2	636.3	14.8	904.7	9.6	9.6	160.0
Second-Plan period	683.9	11.7	1687.4	34.7	2371.2	22.2	23.0	383.4

SOURCE: *Imports of Pakistan: Growth and Structure—A Statistical Study*, Nurul Islam, September 1967, Pakistan Institute of Development Economics.

TABLE 24

REGIONAL NET INFLOW/OUTFLOW OF RESOURCES: PAKISTAN

Annual Average

+ inflow — outflow

Period	East Pakistan		West Pakistan		Pakistan		Disparity	
	Total (Rs. million)	Per capita (Rs.)	Total (Rs. million)	Per capita (Rs.)	Total (Rs. million)	Per capita (Rs.)	Per capita (Rs.)	Index (percentages)
Pre-Plan period	−280.6	−6.2	+56.9	+1.5	−223.7	−2.7	—	—
First-Plan period	−82.2	−1.6	+436.1	+1.0	+353.8	+3.7	—	—
Second-Plan period	+347.5	+5.9	+517.0	+31.2	+1864.5	+17.4	25.3	100.0
Third-Plan period	+399.8	+6.2	+1275.4	+23.7	+1675.3	+14.2	15.6	61.7

NOTE: Regional Net Inflow/outflow of Resources: Exports (including exports to other wing) less Imports (including imports from other wing).

SOURCE: Same as in Tables 16 and 22.

TABLE 25

DISTRIBUTION OF INTER-REGIONAL EXPORTS: PAKISTAN

Annual Average

Plan period	East Pakistan		West Pakistan		Pakistan		Disparity	
	Total (Rs. million)	Per capita (Rs.)	Total (Rs. million)	Per capita (Rs.)	Total (Rs. million)	Per capita (Rs.)	Per capita (Rs.)	Index (percentage)
Pre-Plan period	98.9	2.2	242.3	6.4	341.2	4.1	4.2	100.0
First-Plan period	271.7	5.3	544.2	12.7	815.9	8.7	7.4	176.2
Second-Plan period	452.1	7.8	848.7	17.5	1300.8	12.2	9.7	230.9
Third-Plan period	784.1	11.9	1314.7	23.8	2098.8	17.3	11.9	283.3

SOURCE: Same as Table 16.

APPENDIX

SELECT BIBLIOGRAPHY TO P.C. JOSHI'S PAPER, "LAND REFORM: AN URGENT PROBLEM IN BANGLA DESH"

1. P.C. Joshi, "Land Reform and Agrarian Change in India and Pakistan Since 1947," in Ratna Dutta and P.C. Joshi (Eds.), *Studies in Asian Social Development*, Number I, Tata McGaw-Hill Publishing Company Limited, 1971.
2. J.H. Broomefield, *Elite Conflict in a Plural Society*, University of California Press, Berkeley and Los Angeles, 1968.
3. Gunnar Myrdal, *Asian Drama, An Enquiry Into The Poverty of Nations*, Vols. I, II & III, Allen Lane, The Penguin Press, London, 1968.
4. J. Russell Andrus and Azizali F. Mohammed, *The Economy of Pakistan*, Oxford University Press, London, 1958.
5. O.H.K. Spate and A.T.A. Learmonth, *India and Pakistan: A General and Regional Geography*, Methuen, 1967.
6. Nafis Ahmad, *An Economic Geography of East Pakistan*, Oxford University Press, London, 1958.
7. A.F.A. Husain, *Human and Social Impact of Technological Change in Pakistan*, Vols. I and II, Oxford University Press, Pakistan, 1956.
8. S.M. Hafeez Zaidi, *The Village Culture in Transition: A Study of East Pakistan Rural Society*, East-West Centre Press, Honolulu, 1970.
9. Government of India, Ministry of External Affairs, *Bangla Desh Documents*, New Delhi, 1971.
10. Peoples Republic of Bangla Desh, *Bangla Desh Contemporary Events and Documents*, 1971.
11. Government of Pakistan, Planning Commission, *The Third Five Year Plan—1965-70*, June 1965.
12. Mahbub-ul Haq, *The Strategy of Economic Planning: A Case Study of Pakistan*, Oxford University Press, Pakistan, 1963.
13. United Nations' Food and Agriculture Organization, Rome, *Report on the 1960 World Census of Agriculture*, Vol. I, Part A, Census Results by Countries, Rome, 1966.
14. Kingsley Davis, *The Population of India and Pakistan*, Princeton University Press, 1951.
15. K.N. Raj, *India, Pakistan and China—Economic Growth and Outlook*, Allied Publishers, 1967.
16. Iftikhar Ahmed and John F. Timmons, "Current Land Reforms in East Pakistan," in *Land Economics*, Vol. XLVII, Number I, February 1971.
17. D.R. Mankekar, *Colonialism In East Bengal*, New Delhi, 1971.
18. U.S. Department of Agriculture, *Changes in Agriculture in 26 Developing Nations 1948 to 1963*, Foreign Agricultural Economic Report No. 27, Economic Research Service, November 1965.

19. United Nations' Food and Agriculture Organization, *Progress in Land Reform: Fifth Report*, New York, 1970.
20. East Pakistan Bureau of Statistics, *Statistical Digest of East Pakistan*, Dacca, 1965.
21. East Pakistan Bureau of Statistics, *Statistical Digest of East Pakistan*, Dacca, 1966.

INDEX